PIANO · VOCAL · GUITAR

LOVE SONGS OF
THE BEATLES 2ND EDITION

W9-ASE-157

ISBN 978-0-7935-2504-1

Hal•LEONARD®
CORPORATION

7777 W. BLUEMOUND RD. P.O. BOX 13819 MILWAUKEE, WI 53213

For all works contained herein:
Unauthorized copying, arranging, adapting, recording, Internet posting, public performance,
or other distribution of the printed music in this publication is an infringement of copyright.
Infringers are liable under the law.

Visit Hal Leonard Online at
www.halleonard.com

ALL MY LOVING

Words and Music by JOHN LENNON
and PAUL McCARTNEY

Copyright © 1963, 1964 Sony/ATV Music Publishing LLC
Copyright Renewed
All Rights Administered by Sony/ATV Music Publishing LLC, 8 Music Square West, Nashville, TN 37203
International Copyright Secured   All Rights Reserved

while I'm a - way, ___ I'll write home ev - 'ry day ___

___ and I'll send all my lov - ing ___ to

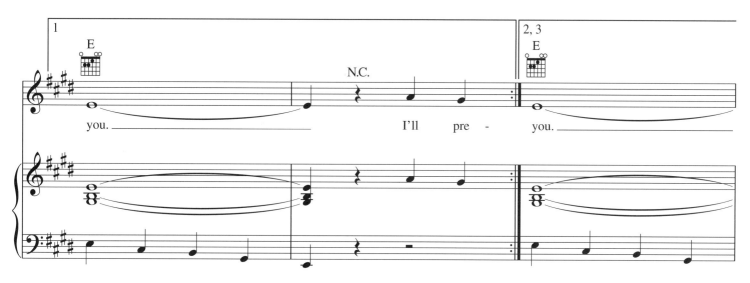

you. ___ I'll pre - you. ___

___ All my lov - ing ___ I ___ will send to

you, _____ all ___ my lov - ing, _____ dar -

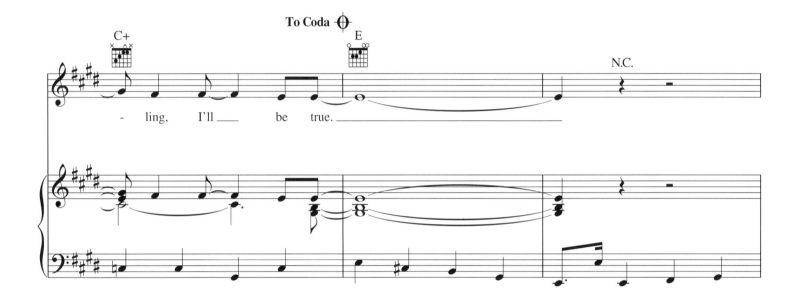

- ling, I'll ___ be true. _____

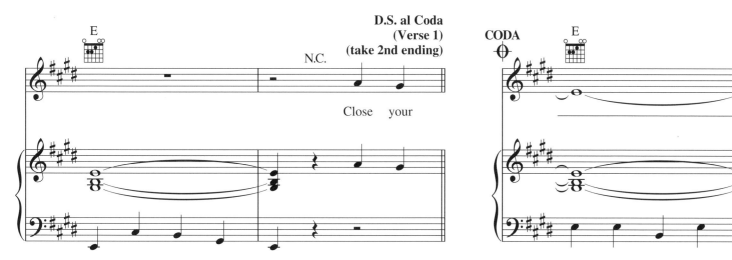

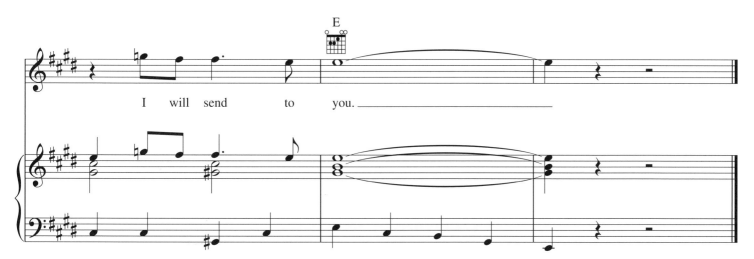

ALL YOU NEED IS LOVE

Words and Music by JOHN LENNON
and PAUL McCARTNEY

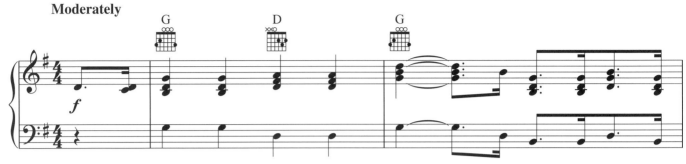

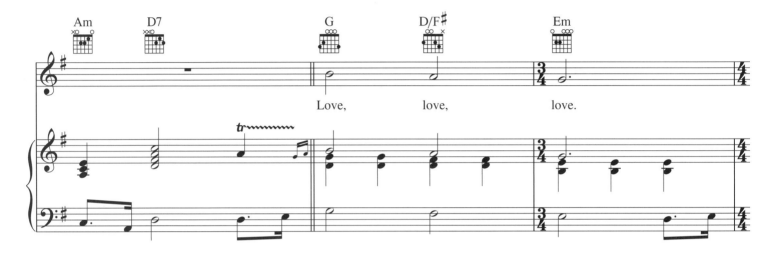

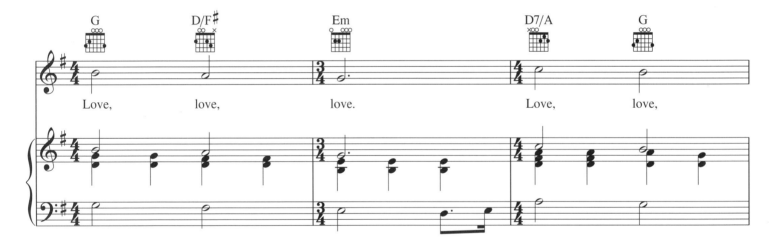

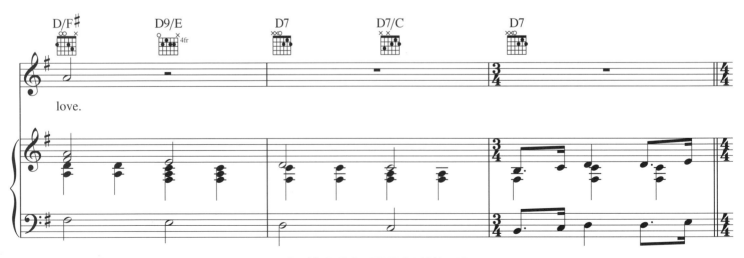

Copyright © 1967 Sony/ATV Music Publishing LLC
Copyright Renewed
All Rights Administered by Sony/ATV Music Publishing LLC, 8 Music Square West, Nashville, TN 37203
International Copyright Secured   All Rights Reserved

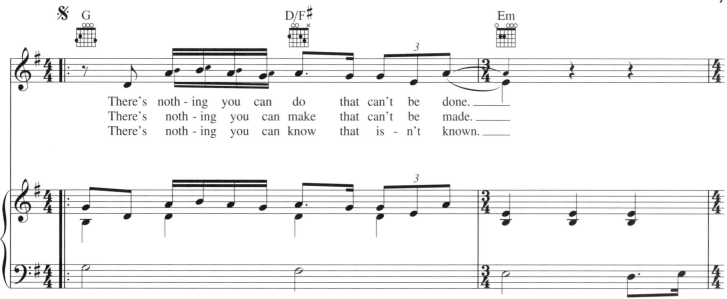

There's noth-ing you can do that can't be done. _____
There's noth-ing you can make that can't be made. _____
There's noth-ing you can know that is-n't known. _____

Noth-ing you can sing that can't be sung. _____
No one you can save that can't be saved. _____
Noth-ing you can see that is-n't shown. _____

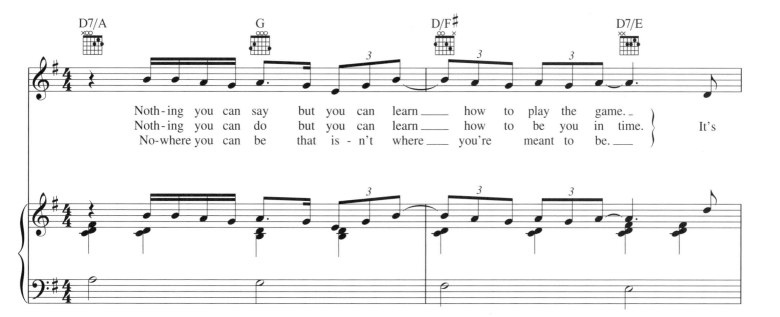

Noth-ing you can say but you can learn _____ how to play the game. __
Noth-ing you can do but you can learn _____ how to be you in time. __
No-where you can be that is-n't where _____ you're meant to be. _____ It's

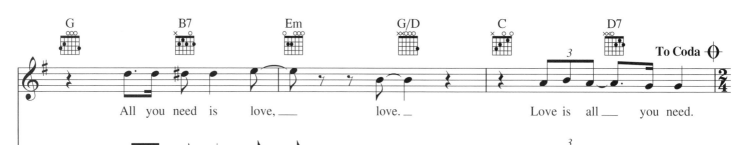

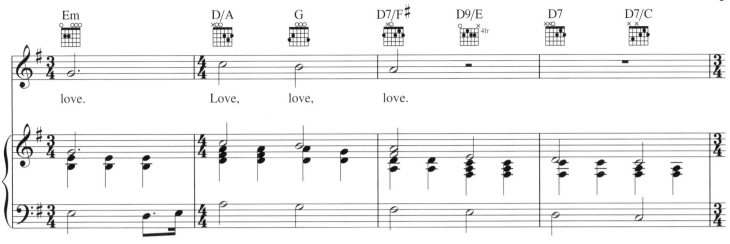

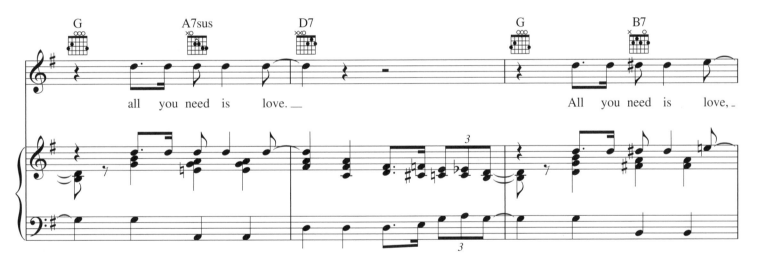

All you need is love. ___ All to-geth-er now. ___

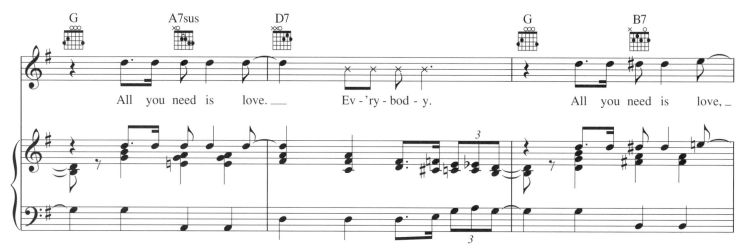

All you need is love. ___ Ev-'ry-bod-y. All you need is love, ___

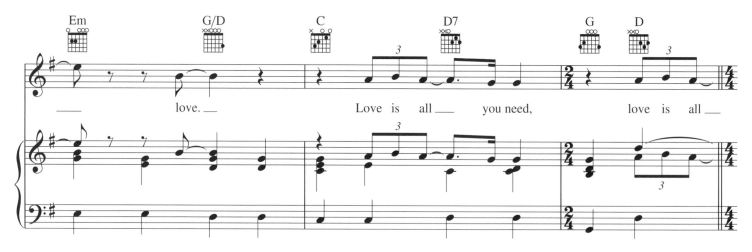

___ love. ___ Love is all ___ you need, love is all ___

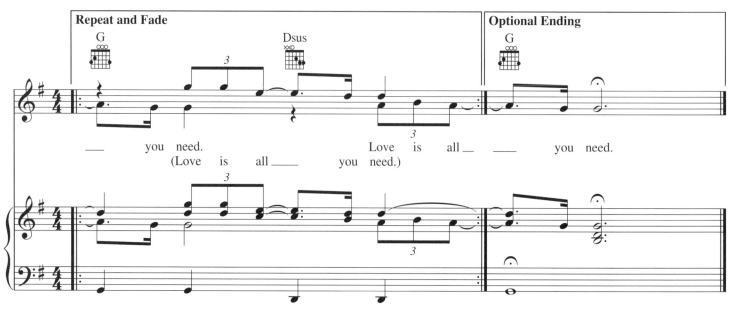

Repeat and Fade **Optional Ending**

___ you need. Love is all ___ ___ you need.
(Love is all ___ you need.)

BECAUSE

Words and Music by JOHN LENNON
and PAUL McCARTNEY

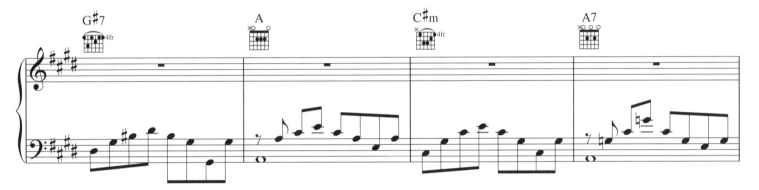

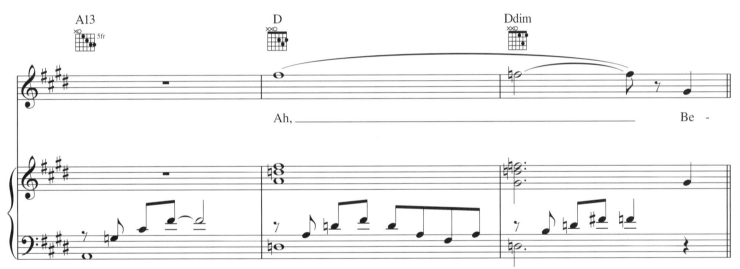

Copyright © 1969 Sony/ATV Music Publishing LLC
Copyright Renewed
All Rights Administered by Sony/ATV Music Publishing LLC, 8 Music Square West, Nashville, TN 37203
International Copyright Secured   All Rights Reserved

be - cause _____ the world _____ is
be - cause _____ the wind _____ is
be - cause _____ the sky _____ is

round. _____ Ah. _____
high. _____ Ah. _____
blue. _____

_____ Be - _____ Love is old, love is new;

love is all, love is you. Be -

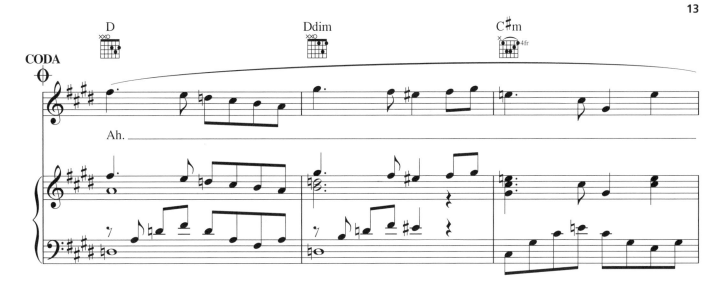

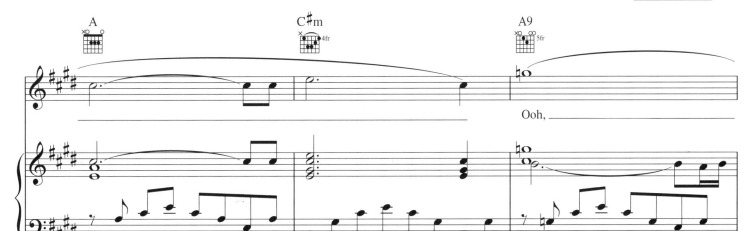

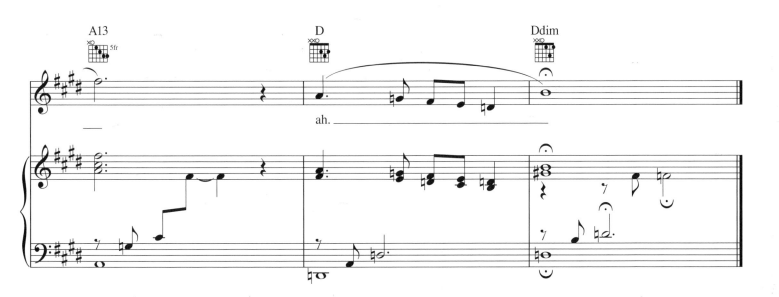

AND I LOVE HER

Words and Music by JOHN LENNON
and PAUL McCARTNEY

Moderately

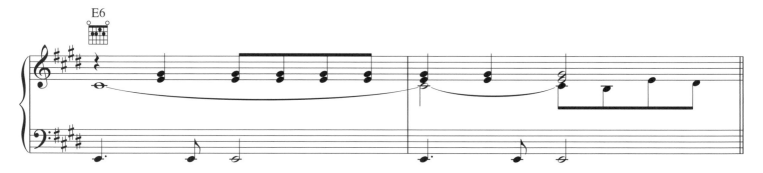

I give her all ____ my love, ____
She gives me ev - 'ry - thing ____
Bright are the stars ____ that shine, ____

that's all I do. ____
and ten - der - ly. ____
dark is the sky. ____

Copyright © 1964 Sony/ATV Music Publishing LLC
Copyright Renewed
All Rights Administered by Sony/ATV Music Publishing LLC, 8 Music Square West, Nashville, TN 37203
International Copyright Secured   All Rights Reserved

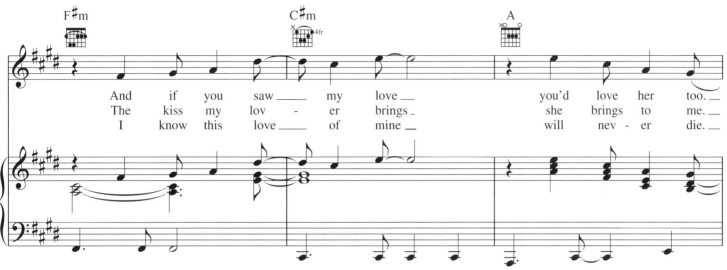

And if you saw ___ my love ___ you'd love her too. ___
The kiss my lov - er brings ___ she brings to me. ___
I know this love ___ of mine ___ will nev - er die. ___

___ I love ___ her.
___ And I love ___ her.
___ And I love ___ her.

To Coda

A love like ours ___

could nev - er die ___ as long as I ___

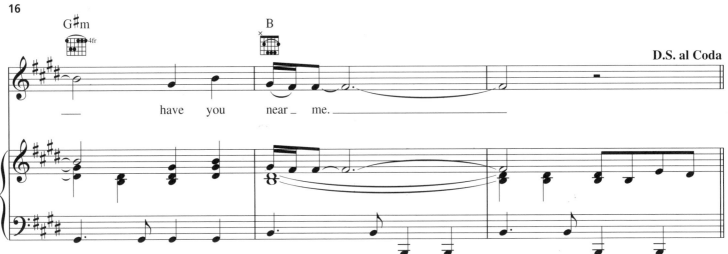

D.S. al Coda

have you near me.

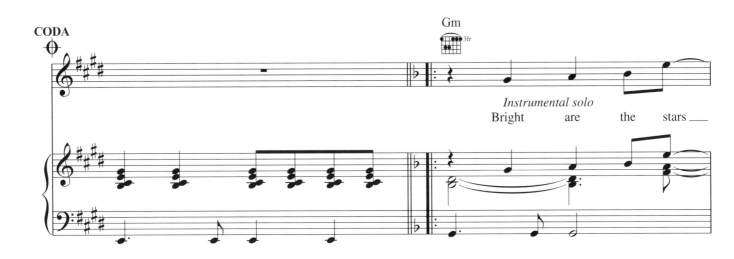

CODA

Instrumental solo

Bright are the stars

that shine, dark is the sky.

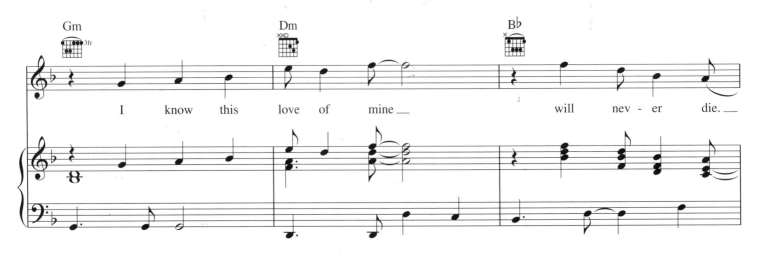

I know this love of mine will nev-er die.

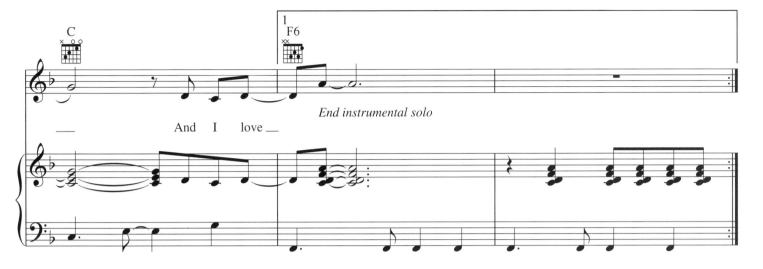

End instrumental solo

And I love

her.

EIGHT DAYS A WEEK

Words and Music by JOHN LENNON
and PAUL McCARTNEY

Brightly, with a Swing feel

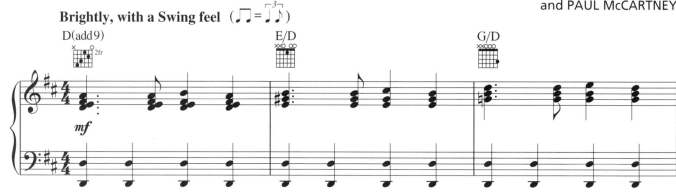

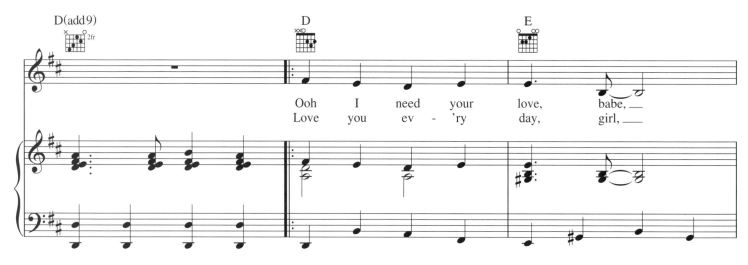

Ooh I need your love, babe, __
Love you ev - 'ry day, girl, __

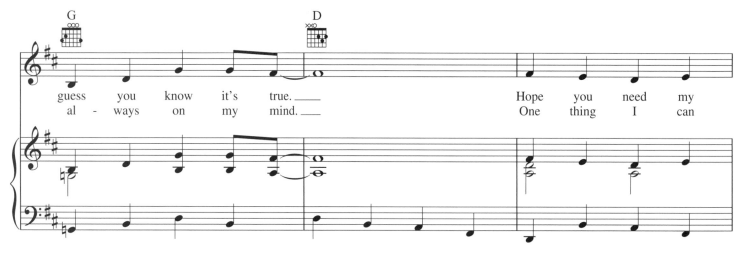

guess you know it's true. __
al - ways on my mind. __

Hope you need my
One thing I can

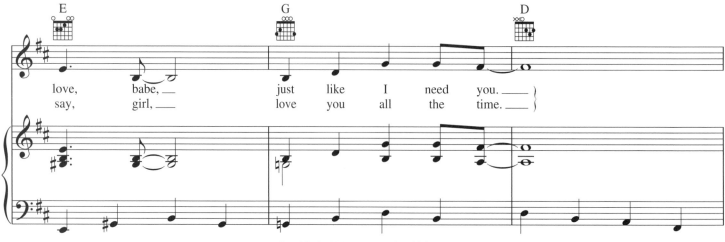

love, babe, __ just like I need you. __
say, girl, __ love you all the time. __

Copyright © 1964 Sony/ATV Music Publishing LLC
Copyright Renewed
All Rights Administered by Sony/ATV Music Publishing LLC, 8 Music Square West, Nashville, TN 37203
International Copyright Secured   All Rights Reserved

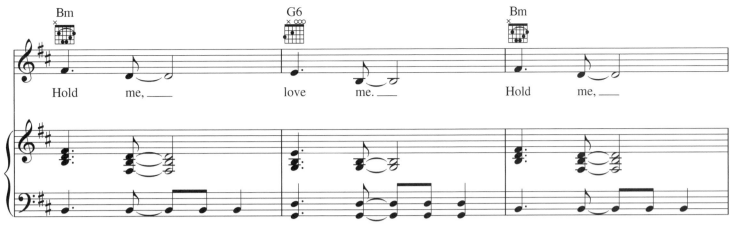

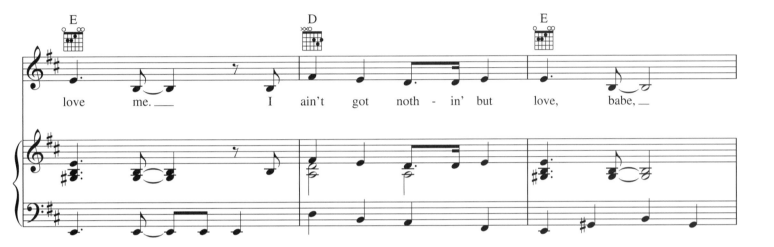

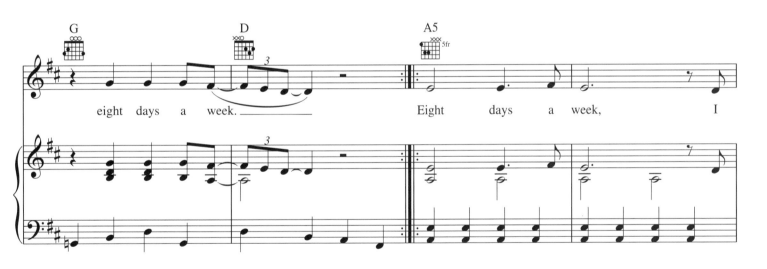

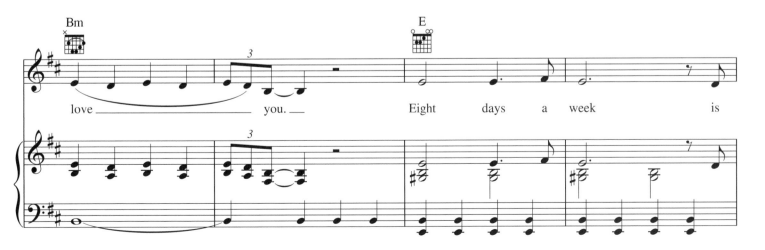

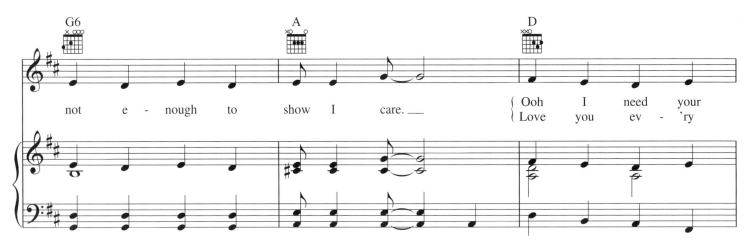

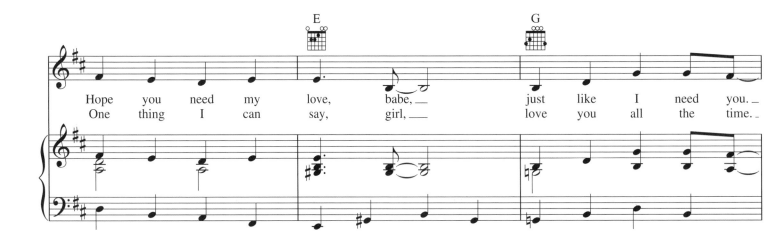

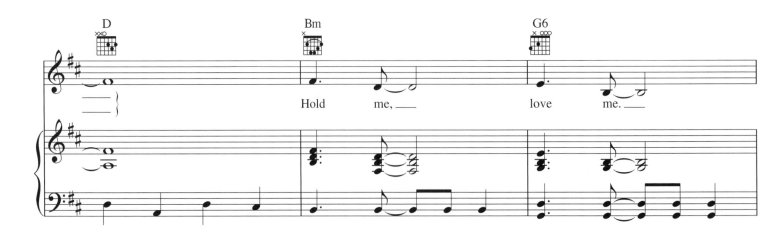

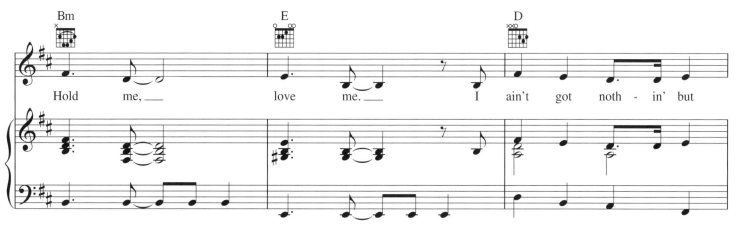

Hold me, __ love me. __ I ain't got noth - in' but

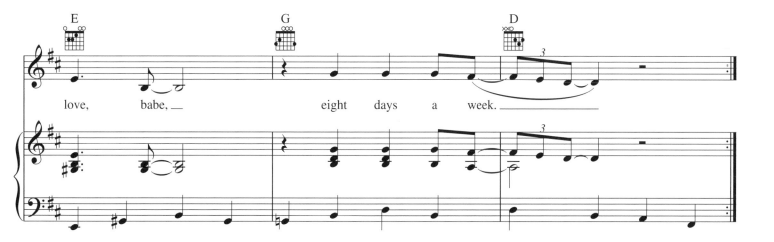

love, babe, __ eight days a week. _____

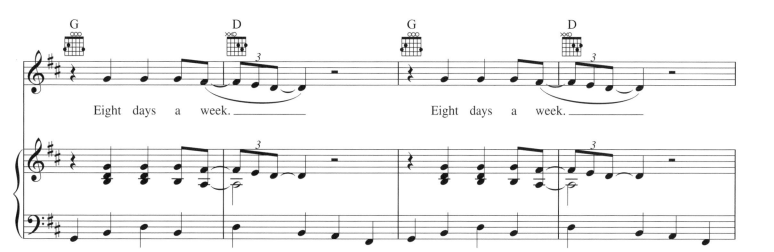

Eight days a week. _____ Eight days a week. _____

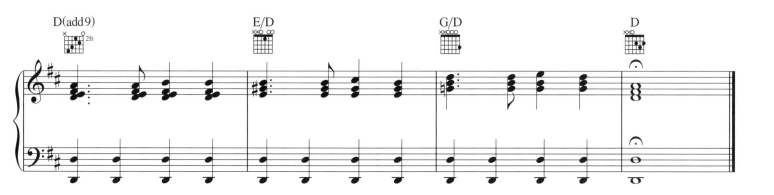

FROM ME TO YOU

Words and Music by JOHN LENNON
and PAUL McCARTNEY

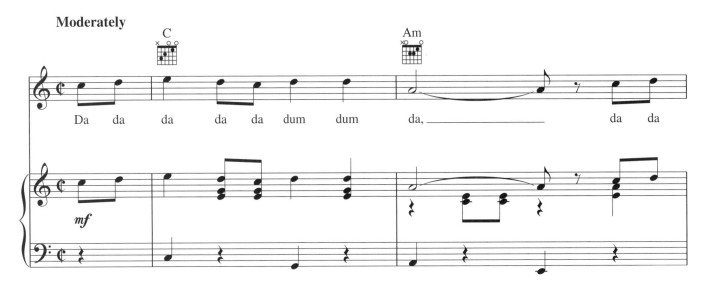

Copyright © 1963 by NORTHERN SONGS LTD., London, England
Copyright Renewed
All rights for the U.S.A., its territories and possessions and Canada assigned to and controlled by GIL MUSIC CORP., 1650 Broadway, New York, NY 10019
International Copyright Secured   All Rights Reserved

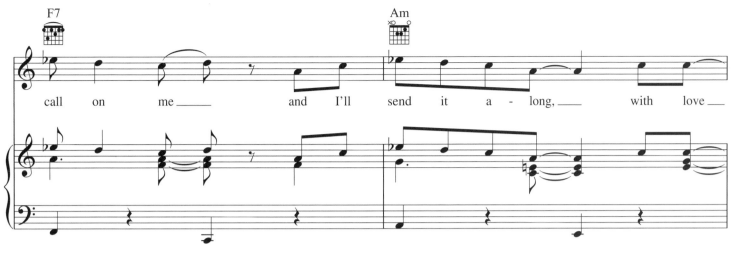

call on me _____ and I'll send it a - long, _____ with love _____

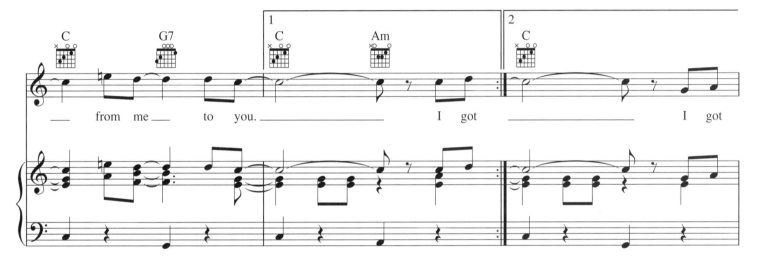

_____ from me ___ to you. _____ I got _____ I got

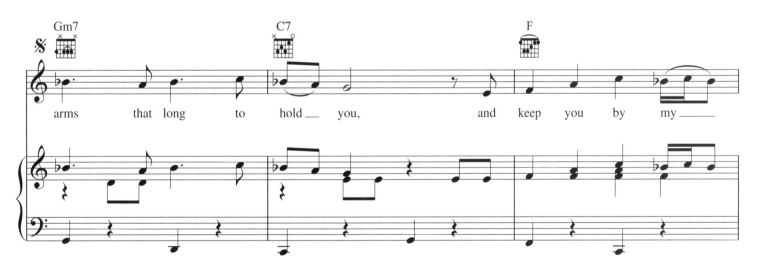

arms that long to hold ___ you, and keep you by my _____

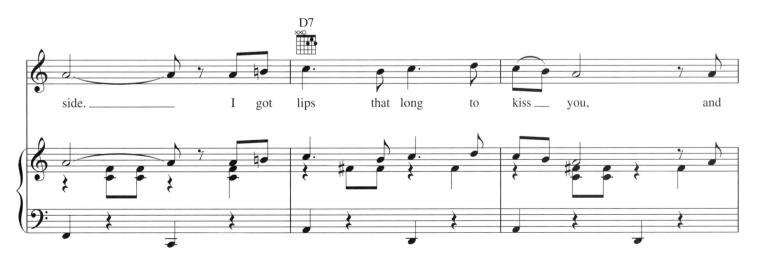

side. _____ I got lips that long to kiss ___ you, and

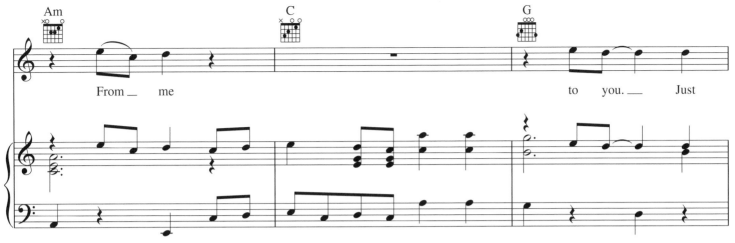

From__ me   to you.__ Just

call on me__ and I'll send it a - long,__ with love__ from me __ to you.__

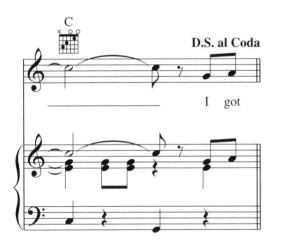

D.S. al Coda

_____ I got

CODA

To you, __   to you, _

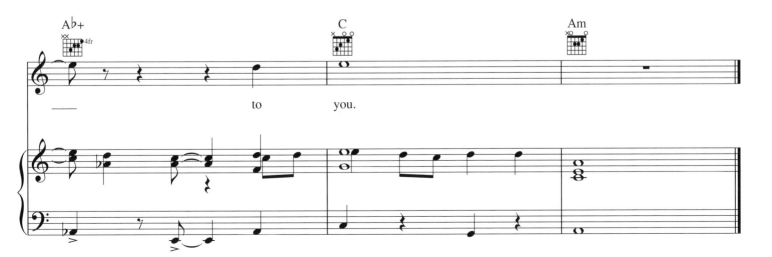

to   you.

GIRL

Words and Music by JOHN LENNON
and PAUL McCARTNEY

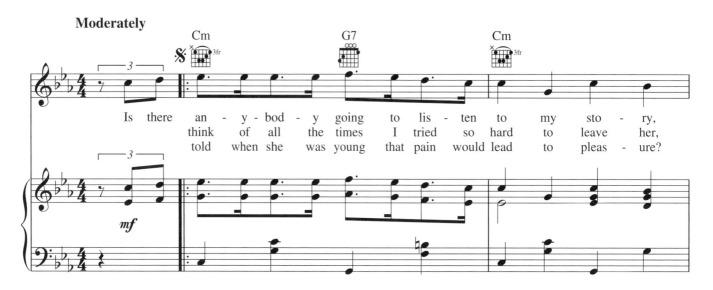

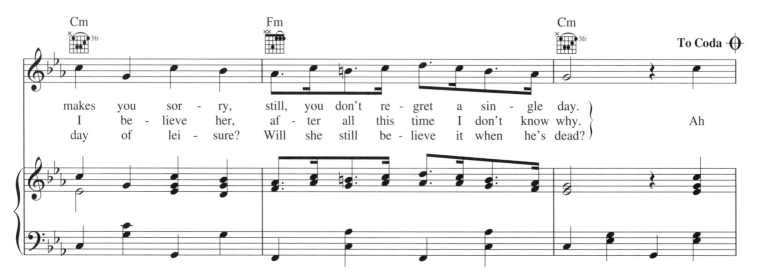

Copyright © 1965 Sony/ATV Music Publishing LLC
Copyright Renewed
All Rights Administered by Sony/ATV Music Publishing LLC, 8 Music Square West, Nashville, TN 37203
International Copyright Secured   All Rights Reserved

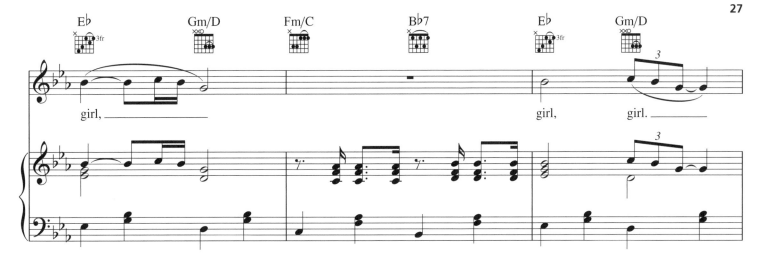

girl, _____ girl, girl. _____

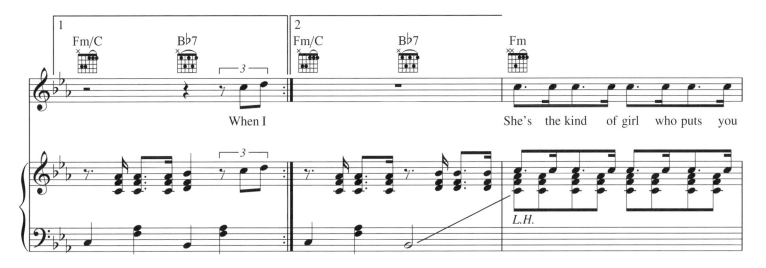

When I

She's the kind of girl who puts you

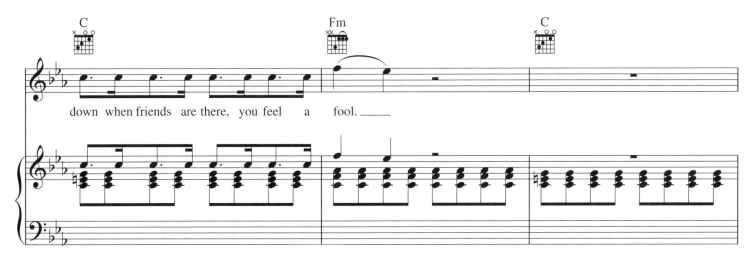

down when friends are there, you feel a fool. _____

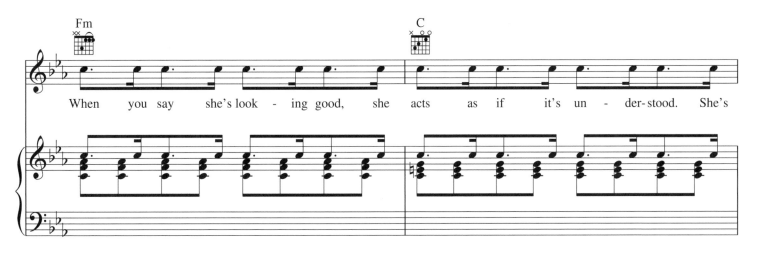

When you say she's look - ing good, she acts as if it's un - der - stood. She's

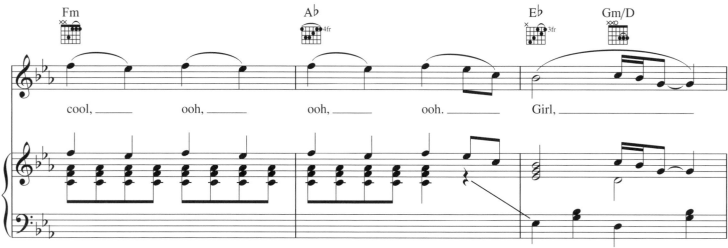

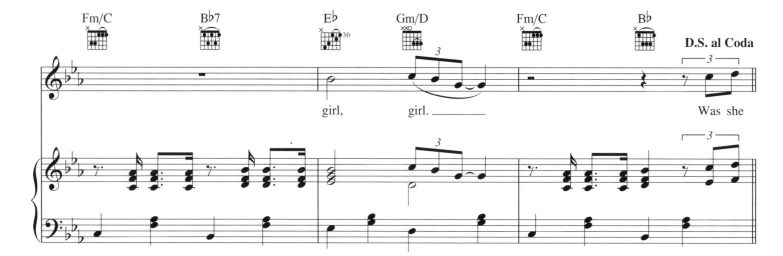

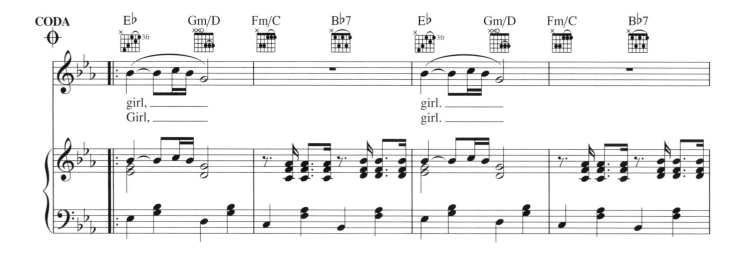

I WILL

Words and Music by JOHN LENNON
and PAUL McCARTNEY

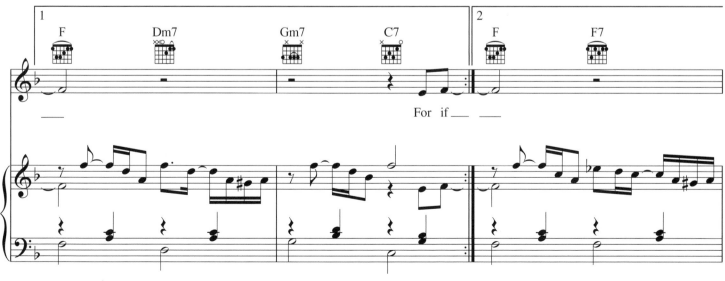

Copyright © 1968 Sony/ATV Music Publishing LLC
Copyright Renewed
All Rights Administered by Sony/ATV Music Publishing LLC, 8 Music Square West, Nashville, TN 37203
International Copyright Secured   All Rights Reserved

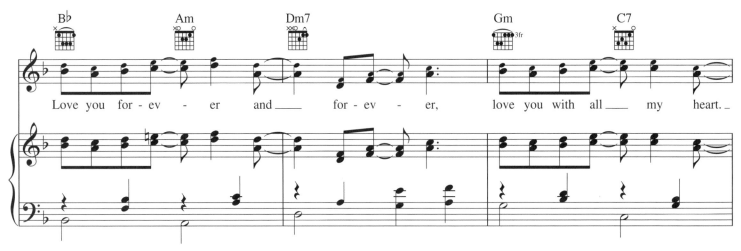

Love you for- ev - er and ___ for - ev - er, love you with all ___ my heart. ___

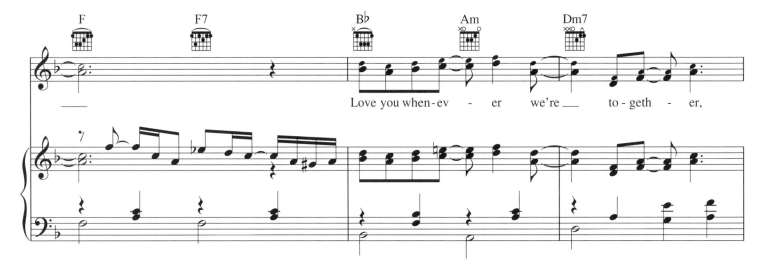

___ Love you when-ev - er we're ___ to - geth - er,

love you when we're ___ a - part. ___ And when ___ at last ___ I find ___

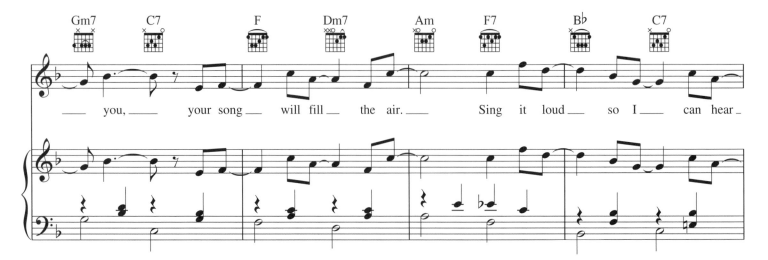

___ you, ___ your song ___ will fill ___ the air. ___ Sing it loud ___ so I ___ can hear ___

you, make it eas - y to be near you, for the things you do en - dear

you to me. Ah, you know I will.

I will.

La la la la la la la la la, la la la la la la la.

HERE, THERE AND EVERYWHERE

Words and Music by JOHN LENNON
and PAUL McCARTNEY

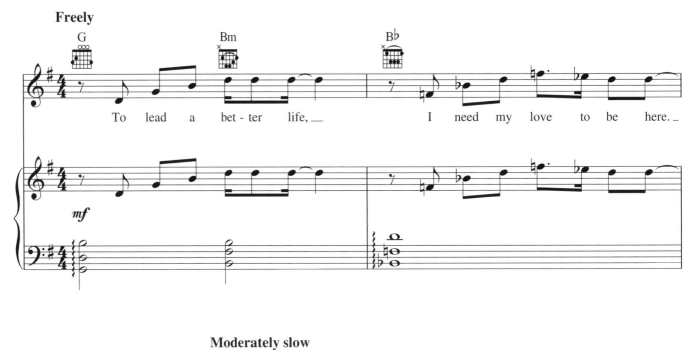

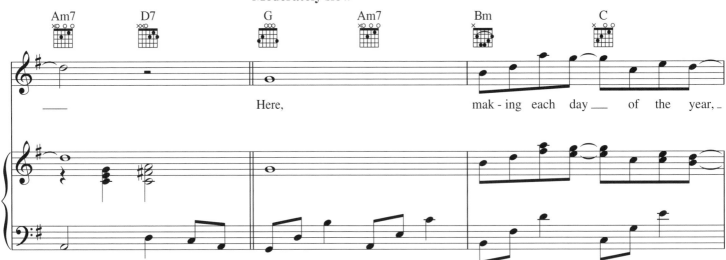

Copyright © 1966 Sony/ATV Music Publishing LLC
Copyright Renewed
All Rights Administered by Sony/ATV Music Publishing LLC, 8 Music Square West, Nashville, TN 37203
International Copyright Secured   All Rights Reserved

No - bod - y can ___ de - ny ___ that there's some - thing there. ___

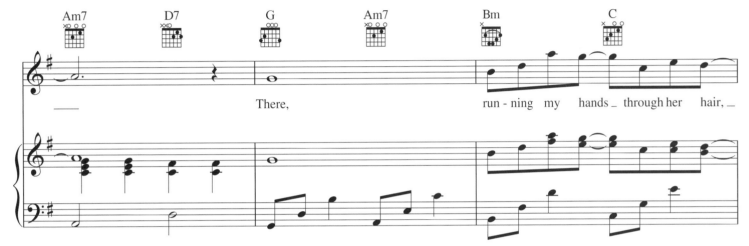

___ There, run - ning my hands ___ through her hair, ___

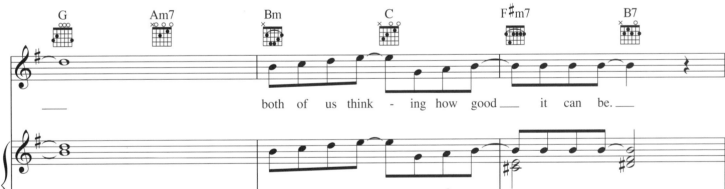

___ both of us think - ing how good ___ it can be. ___

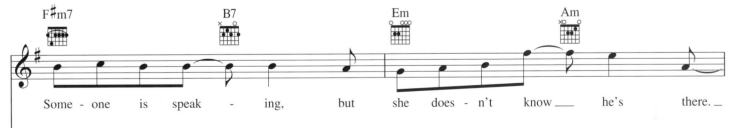

Some - one is speak - ing, but she does - n't know ___ he's there. ___

I want her ev-'ry-where and if

she's be-side me I know I need nev-er care.

But to love her is to need her ev-'ry - where, __

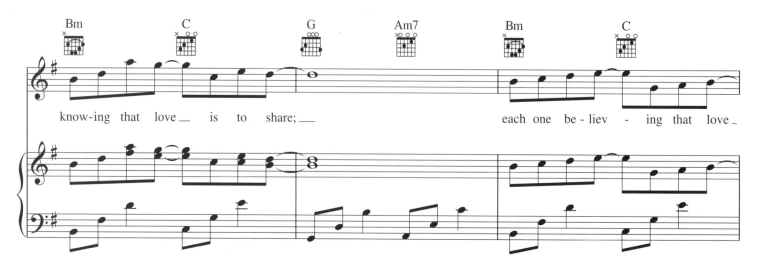

know-ing that love __ is to share; __ each one be-liev - ing that love _

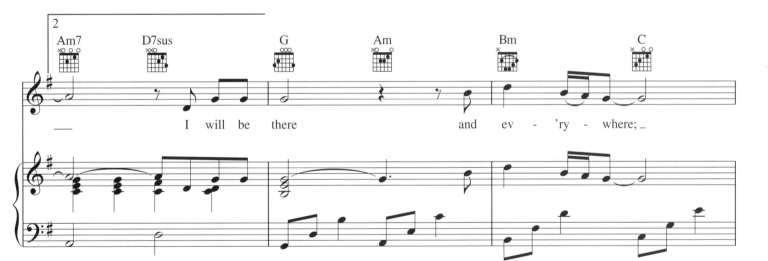

HEY JUDE

Words and Music by JOHN LENNON
and PAUL McCARTNEY

Slowly

Hey Jude,_____ don't make it bad; take a
_____ don't make it bad; take a

sad song _____ and make it bet - ter. _____ Re -
sad song _____ and make it bet - ter. _____ Re -

mem - ber to let her in - to your heart; then you can start ___
mem - ber to let her un - der your skin, then you be - gin ___

Copyright © 1968 Sony/ATV Music Publishing LLC
Copyright Renewed
All Rights Administered by Sony/ATV Music Publishing LLC, 8 Music Square West, Nashville, TN 37203
International Copyright Secured All Rights Reserved

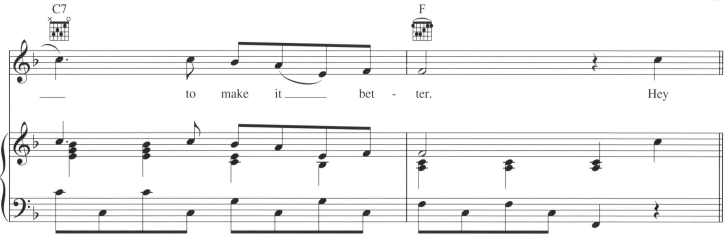

to make it _____ bet - ter. Hey

Jude, _____ don't be a - fraid. You were made to _____ go out and
Jude, _____ don't let me down. You have found her, _____ now go and

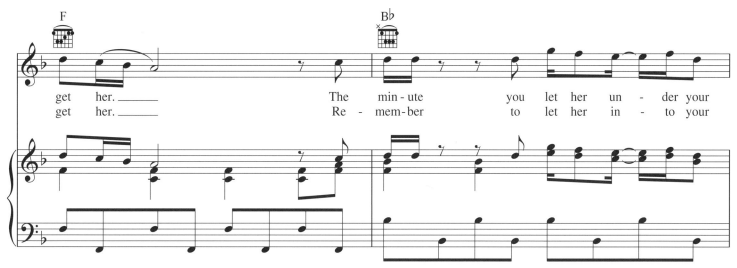

get her. _____ The min - ute you let her un - der your
get her. _____ Re - mem - ber to let her in - to your

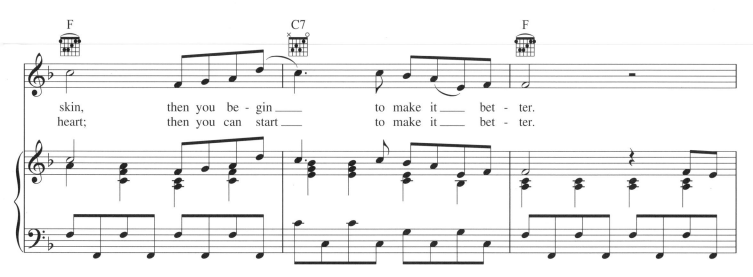

skin, _____ then you be - gin _____ to make it ____ bet - ter.
heart; _____ then you can start _____ to make it ____ bet - ter.

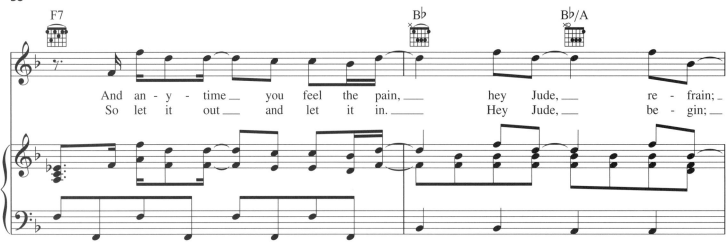

And an - y - time___ you feel the pain,___ hey Jude,___ re - frain;___
So let it out___ and let it in.___ Hey Jude,___ be - gin;___

___ don't car - ry the world___ up - on___ your shoul - ders.___
___ you're wait - ing for some - one to___ per - form___ with.___

For well you know___ that it's a fool___ who plays___ it cool___
And don't you know___ that it's just you?___ Hey Jude,___ you'll do.___

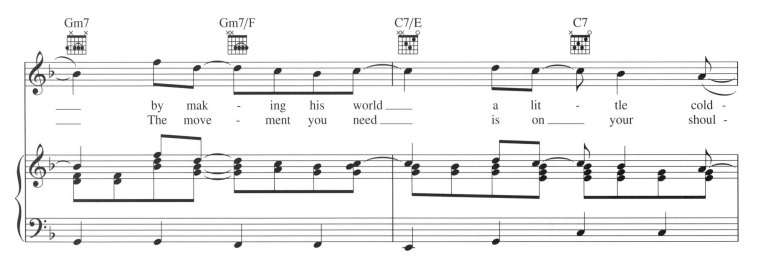

___ by mak - ing his world___ a lit - tle cold -
The move - ment you need___ is on___ your shoul -

I FEEL FINE

Words and Music by JOHN LENNON
and PAUL McCARTNEY

Bright Rock

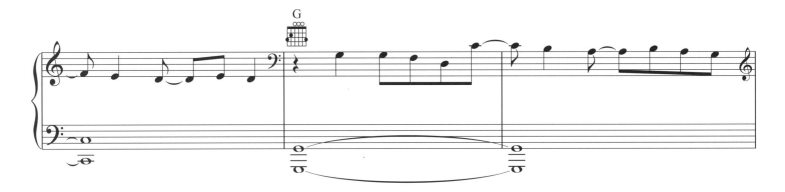

Ba - by's good to me ____
Ba - by says she's mine ____
Ba - by says she's mine ____

____ you know, ____ she's hap - py as can be, ____ you know ____ she
____ you know, ____ she tells me all the time, ____ you know ____ she
____ you know, ____ she tells me all the time, ____ you know ____ she

Copyright © 1964 Sony/ATV Music Publishing LLC
Copyright Renewed
All Rights Administered by Sony/ATV Music Publishing LLC, 8 Music Square West, Nashville, TN 37203
International Copyright Secured   All Rights Reserved

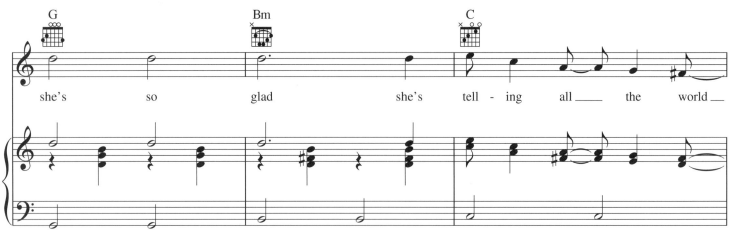

she's   so   glad   she's tell - ing all ___ the world ___

___   that her ba - by buys her things ___ you know, ___ he

buys her dia - mond rings, ___ you know ___ she

said so.   She's in love ___ with

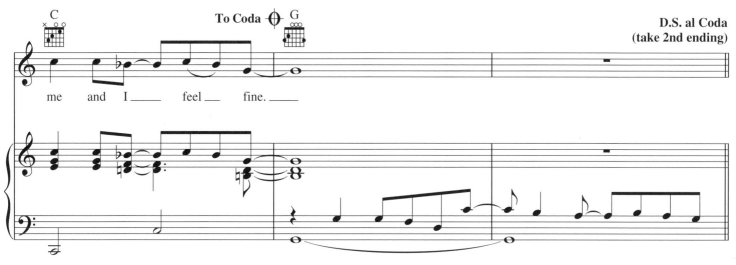

I NEED YOU

Words and Music by
GEORGE HARRISON

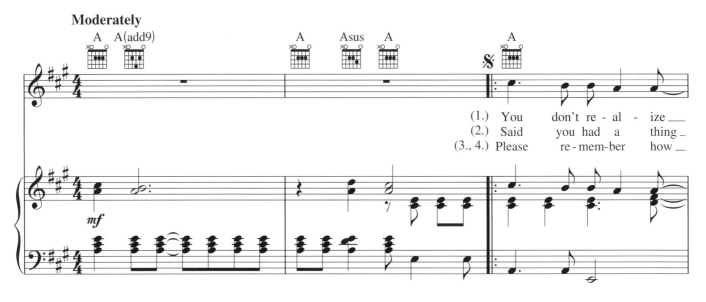

(1.) You don't re-al-ize __
(2.) Said you had a thing __
(3., 4.) Please re-mem-ber how __

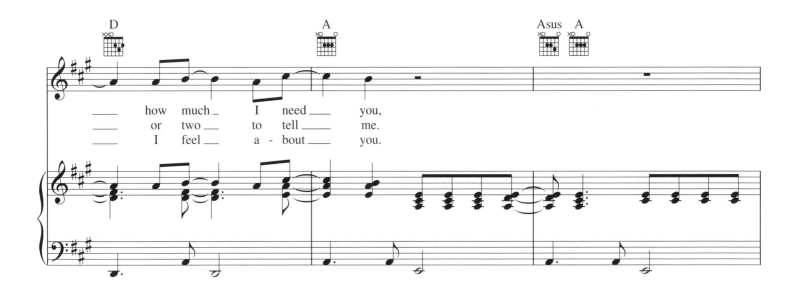

__ how much __ I need __ you,
__ or two __ to tell __ me.
__ I feel __ a-bout __ you.

Love you all the time __ and nev-er leave __ you.
How was I to know __ you would up-set __ me?
I could nev-er real-ly live with-out __ you.

Copyright © 1965 Sony/ATV Music Publishing LLC
Copyright Renewed
All Rights Administered by Sony/ATV Music Publishing LLC, 8 Music Square West, Nashville, TN 37203
International Copyright Secured   All Rights Reserved

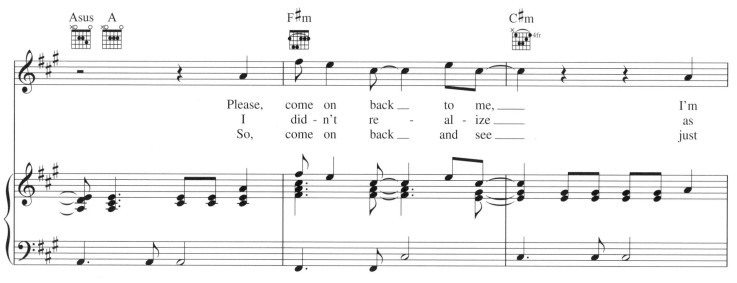

Please, come on back ___ to me, ___ I'm
I did-n't re - al - ize ___ as
So, come on back ___ and see ___ just

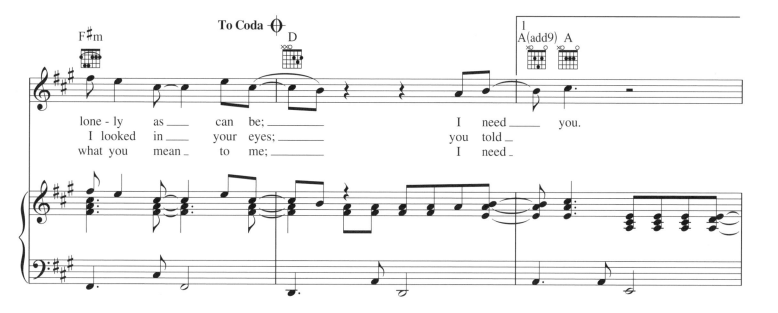

lone - ly as ___ can be; ___ I need ___ you.
I looked in ___ your eyes; ___ you told ___
what you mean ___ to me; ___ I need ___

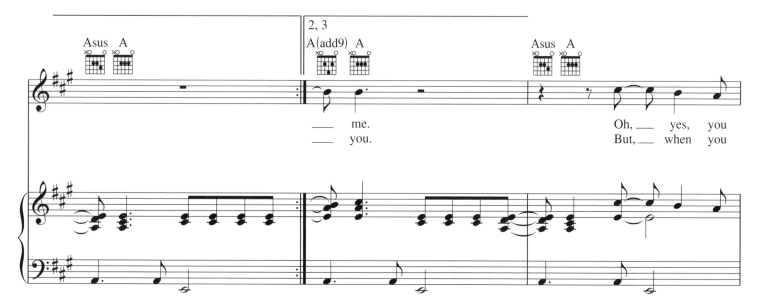

___ me. Oh, ___ yes, you
___ you. But, ___ when you

told me   you   don't want my   lov-in' an - y - more. ___
told me   you   don't want my   lov-in' an - y - more, ___

That's when it   hurt me,   and feel-in' like this,   I
that's when it   hurt me,

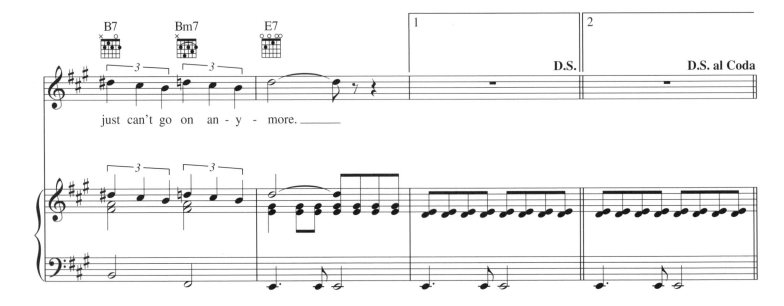

just can't go on an - y - more. ___

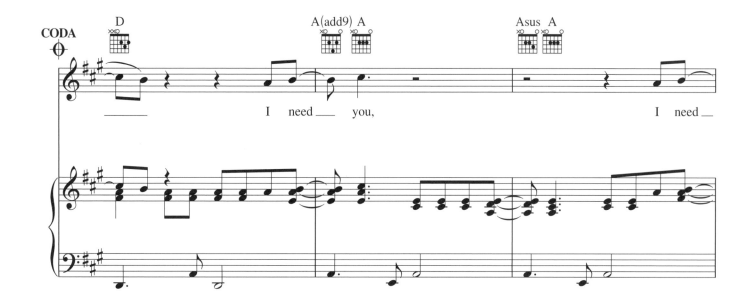

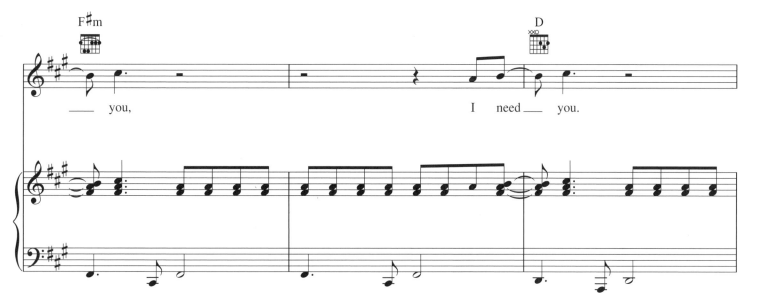

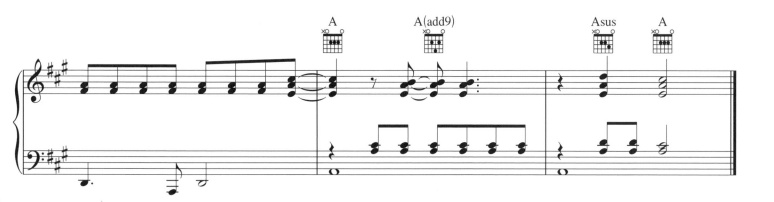

I WANT TO HOLD YOUR HAND

Words and Music by JOHN LENNON
and PAUL McCARTNEY

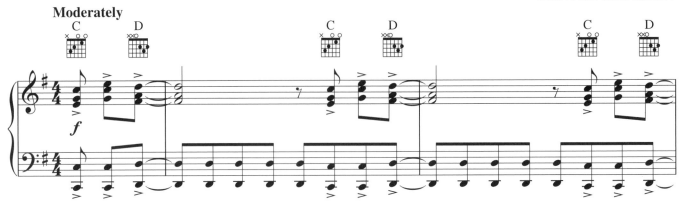

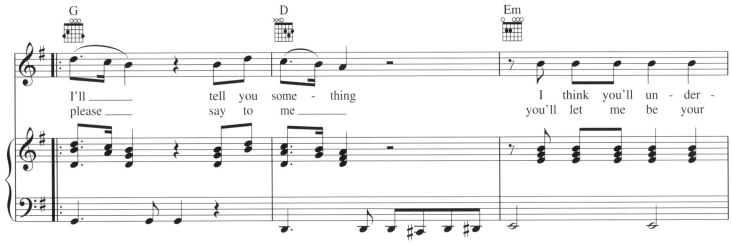

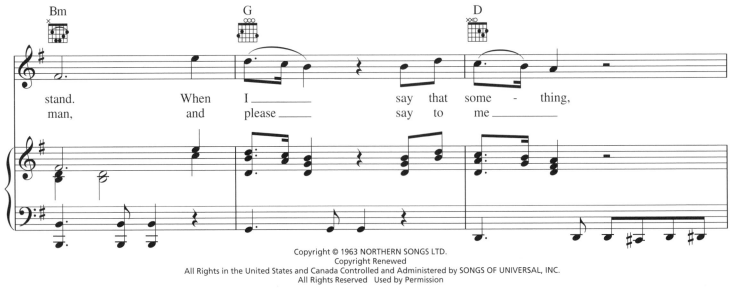

Copyright © 1963 NORTHERN SONGS LTD.
Copyright Renewed
All Rights in the United States and Canada Controlled and Administered by SONGS OF UNIVERSAL, INC.
All Rights Reserved   Used by Permission

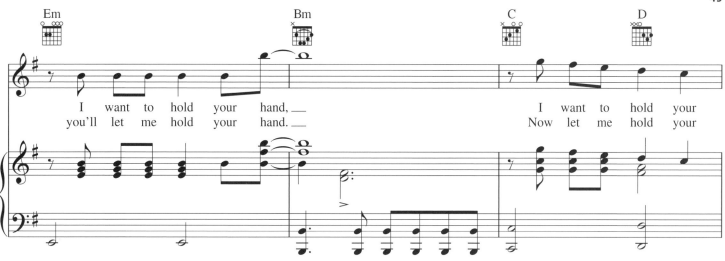

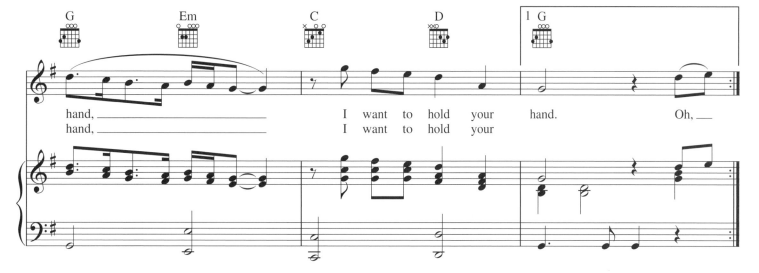

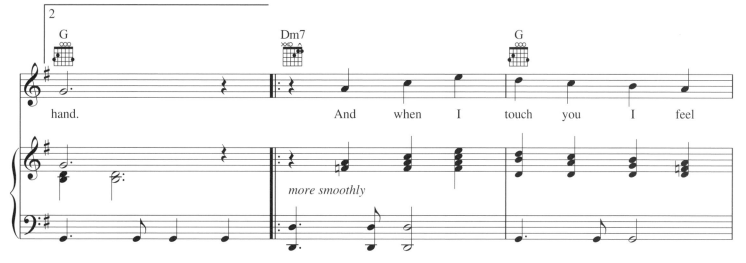

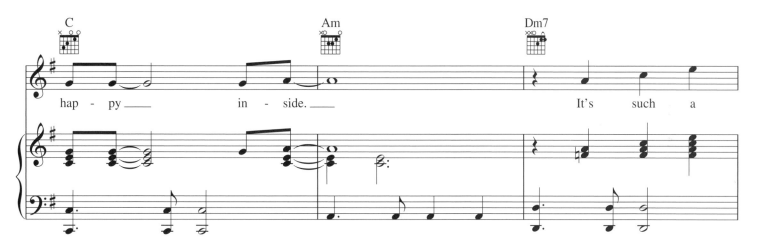

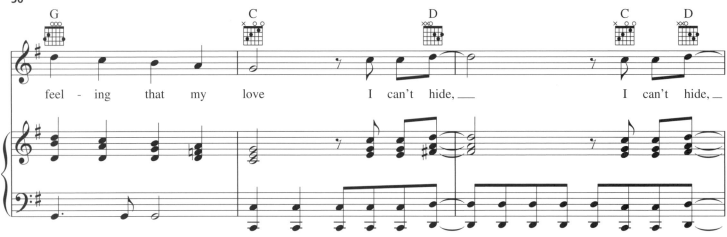

feel - ing that my love I can't hide, ___ I can't hide, ___

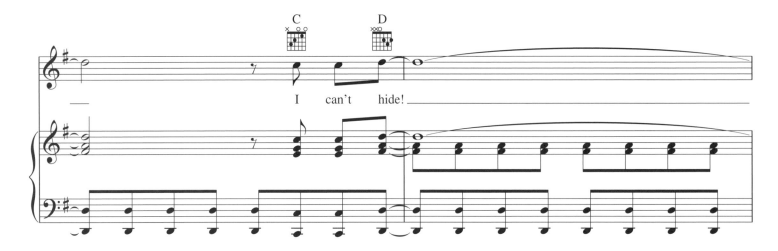

___ I can't hide! _____

{ Yeah, you _____ got that some - thing
{ Yeah, you _____ got that some - thing

as before

I think you'll un - der - stand. When I _____ say that
I think you'll un - der - stand. When I _____ feel that

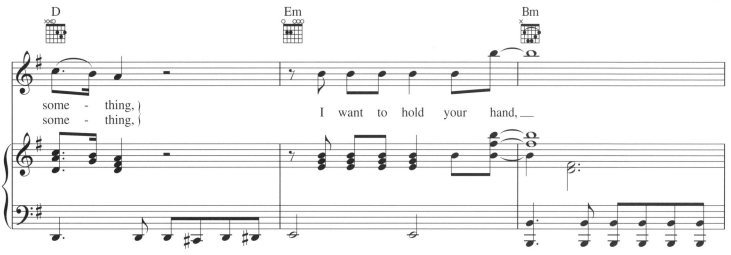

some - thing,)
some - thing,)
I want to hold your hand, __

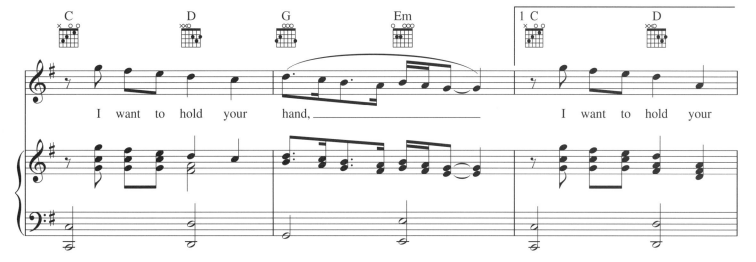

I want to hold your hand, _____ I want to hold your

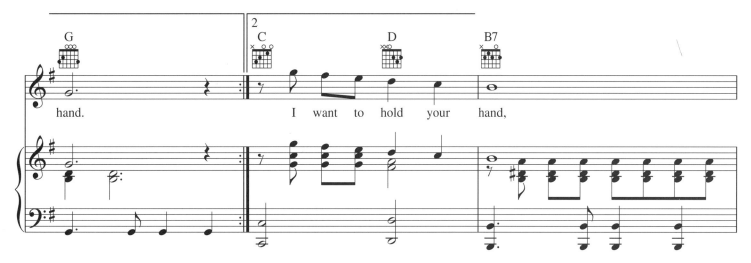

hand.
I want to hold your hand,

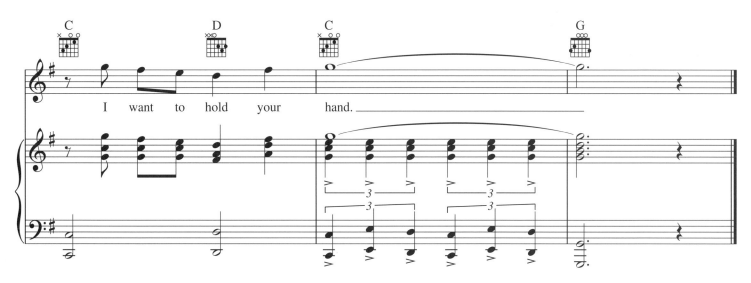

I want to hold your hand. _____

I'M HAPPY JUST TO DANCE WITH YOU

Words and Music by JOHN LENNON
and PAUL McCARTNEY

Moderately

Be-fore this dance is through ___ I think I'll

love you too, ___ I'm so hap-py when you dance with me. I don't

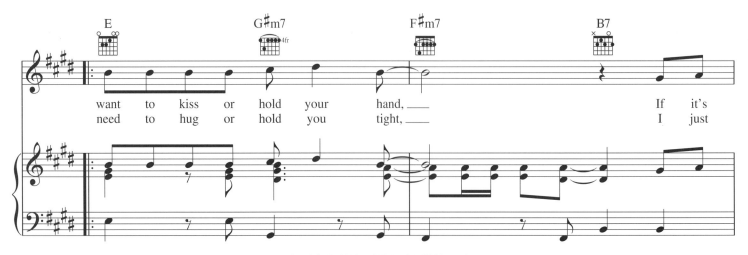

want to kiss or hold your hand, ___ If it's
need to hug or hold you tight, ___ I just

Copyright © 1964 Sony/ATV Music Publishing LLC
Copyright Renewed
All Rights Administered by Sony/ATV Music Publishing LLC, 8 Music Square West, Nashville, TN 37203
International Copyright Secured   All Rights Reserved

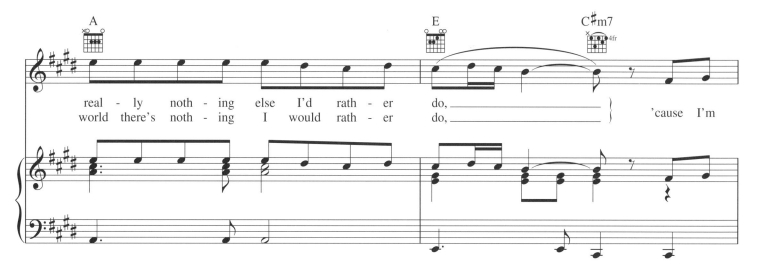

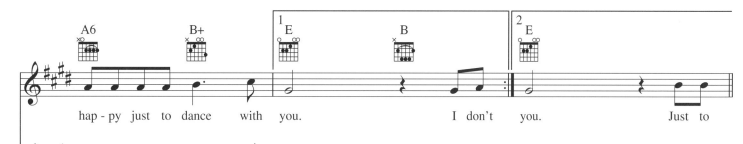

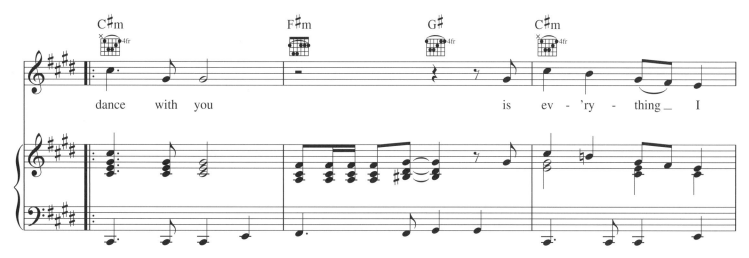

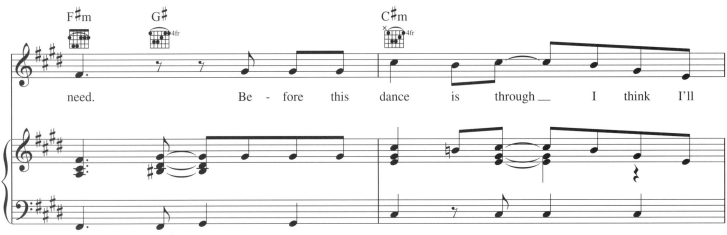

need. Be - fore this dance is through ___ I think I'll

love you too, ___ I'm so hap - py when you dance with me. If some -

bod - y tries to take my place, ___ let's pre -

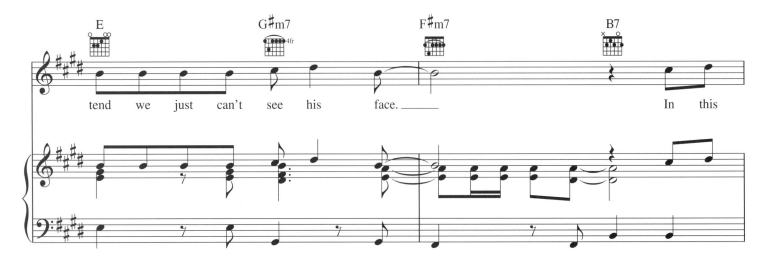

tend we just can't see his face. ___ In this

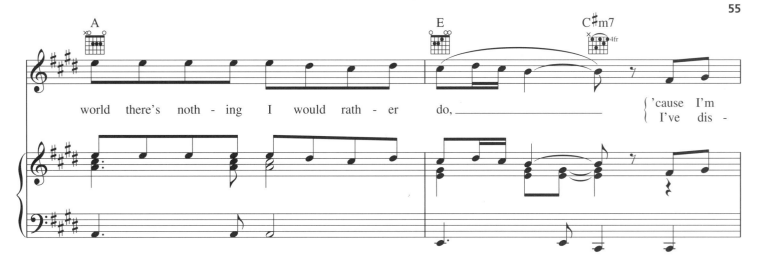

world there's noth-ing I would rath-er do, _____ { 'cause I'm
{ I've dis-

hap-py just to dance with you. Just to

cov-ered I'm in love with you.

'Cause I'm hap-py just to dance with you.

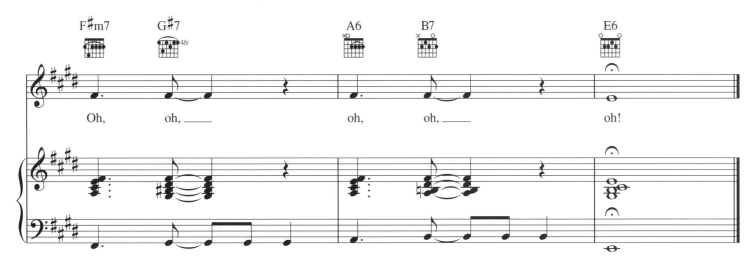

Oh, oh, _____ oh, oh, _____ oh!

IF I FELL

Words and Music by JOHN LENNON
and PAUL McCARTNEY

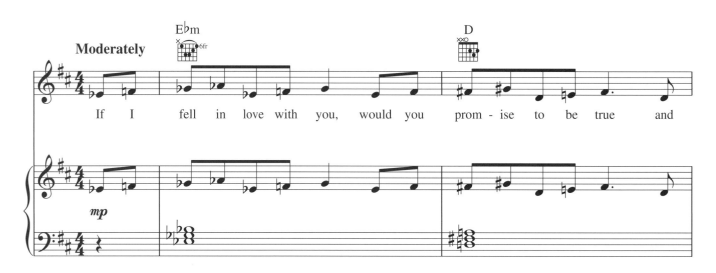

Moderately

If I fell in love with you, would you prom-ise to be true and

help me un-der-stand? 'Cause I've been in love be-fore, and I

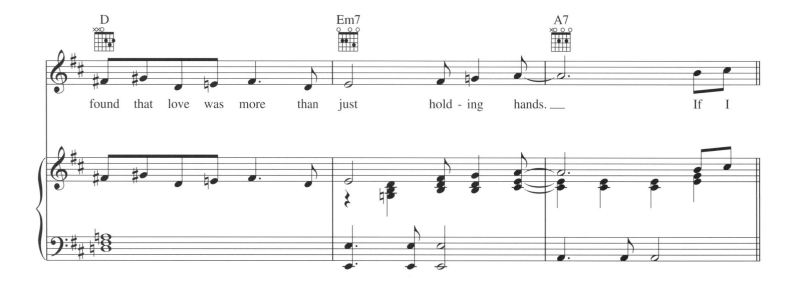

found that love was more than just hold-ing hands. ___ If I

Copyright © 1964 Sony/ATV Music Publishing LLC
Copyright Renewed
All Rights Administered by Sony/ATV Music Publishing LLC, 8 Music Square West, Nashville, TN 37203
International Copyright Secured   All Rights Reserved

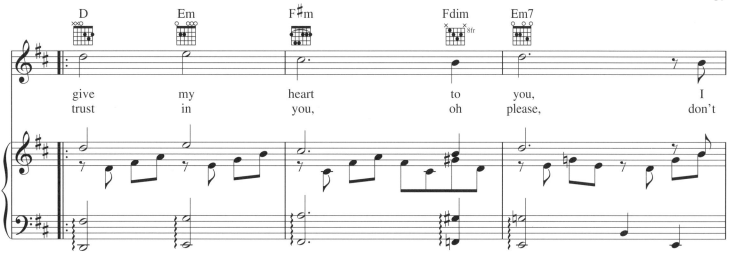

give my heart to you, I
trust in you, oh please, don't

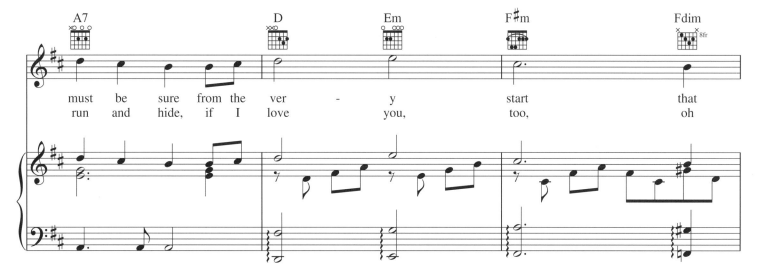

must be sure from the ver - y start that
run and hide, if I love you, too, oh

you would love me more than her.
please, don't hurt my pride like her.

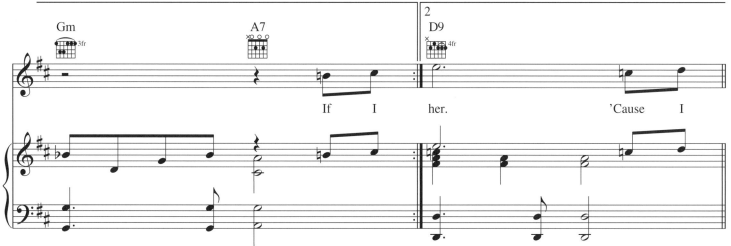

If I her. 'Cause I

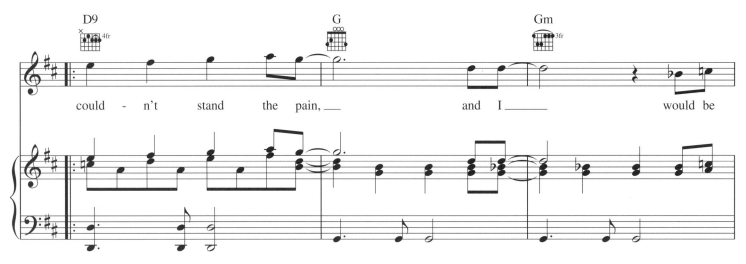

could - n't stand the pain, ___ and I _____ would be

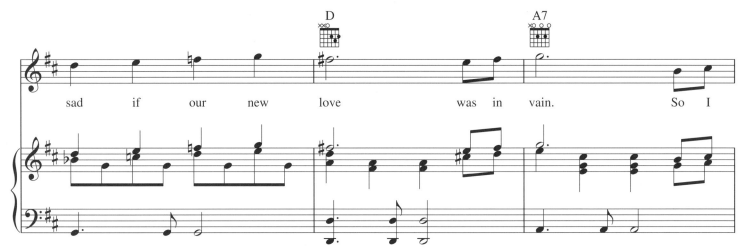

sad if our new love was in vain. So I

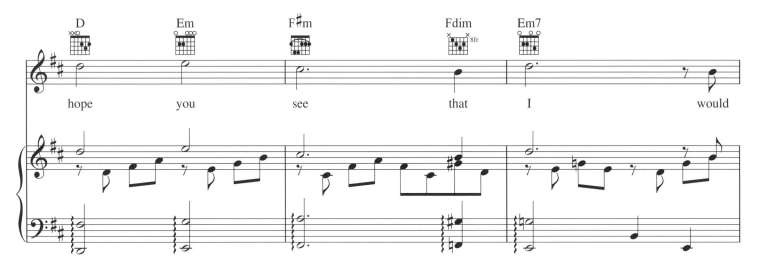

hope you see that I would

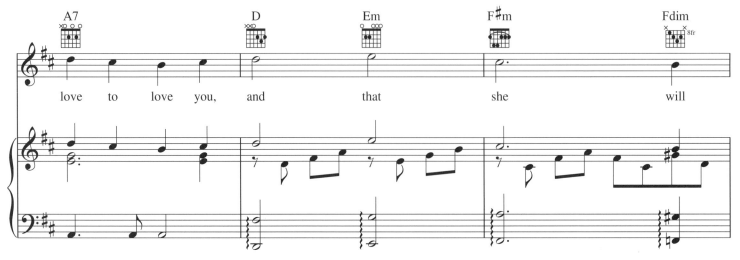

love to love you, and that she will

cry   when she learns we are two. ____   'Cause I

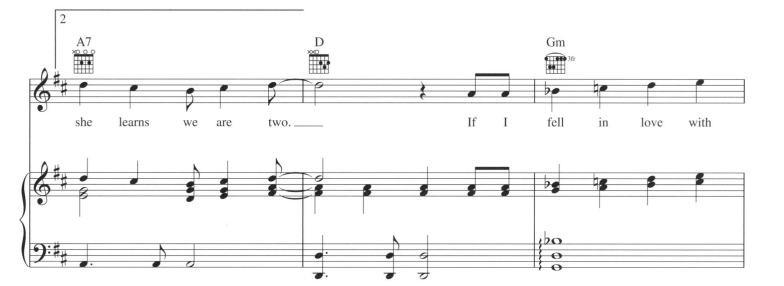

she   learns we are   two. ____   If   I   fell   in   love with

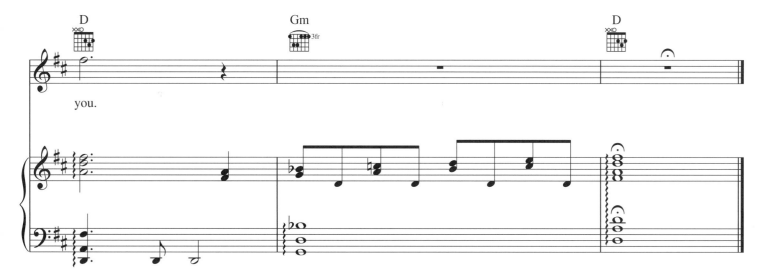

you.

IN MY LIFE

Words and Music by JOHN LENNON
and PAUL McCARTNEY

Moderately

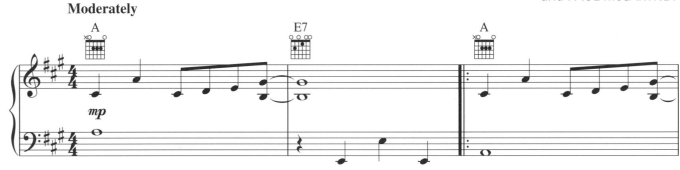

There are plac- es I'll re- mem- ber all my
But of all these friends and lov- ers all there is

life, _____ though some have changed. ___ Some for- ev- er, not for
no _____ one com- pares with you. ___ And these mem- 'ries lose their

bet- ter; some have gone _____ and some re- main. ___ All these
mean- ing when I think of ___ love as some- thing new. ___ Tho' I

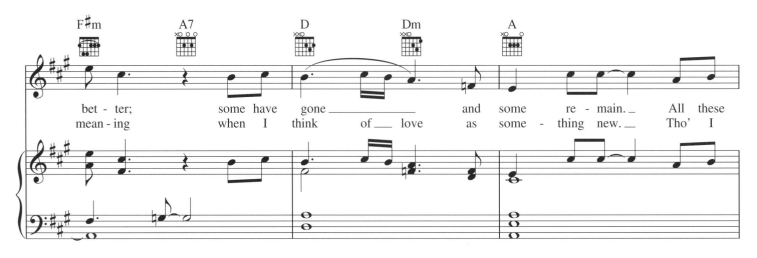

Copyright © 1965 Sony/ATV Music Publishing LLC
Copyright Renewed
All Rights Administered by Sony/ATV Music Publishing LLC, 8 Music Square West, Nashville, TN 37203
International Copyright Secured   All Rights Reserved

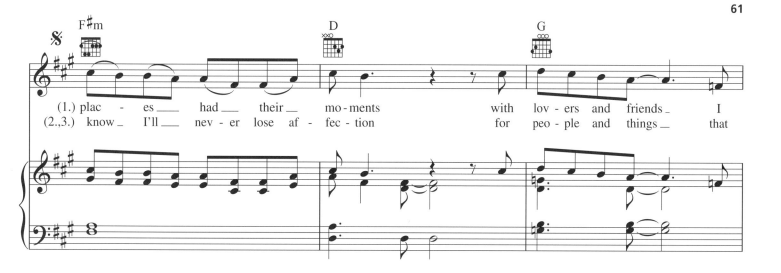

(1.) plac - es ____ had ____ their ____ mo - ments with lov - ers and friends ____ I
(2.,3.) know ____ I'll ____ nev - er lose af - fec - tion for peo - ple and things ____ that

still can re - call. ____ Some are dead ____ and ____ some ____ are ____
went ____ be - fore, ____ I know I'll of - ten stop and think a -

liv - ing, ____ in my ____ life I've loved them all. ____
bout them, _ in my ____ life I love you more. ____

To Coda ⊕

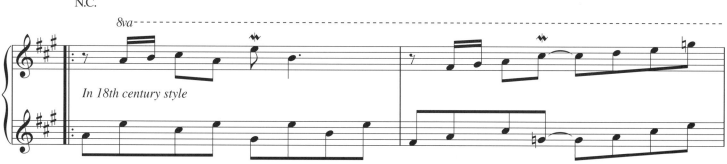

N.C.

In 18th century style

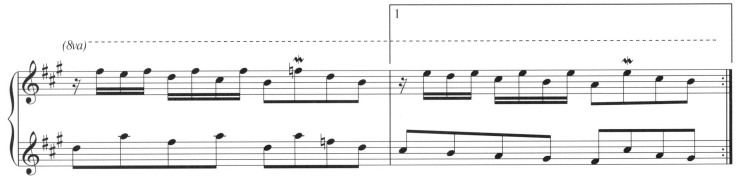

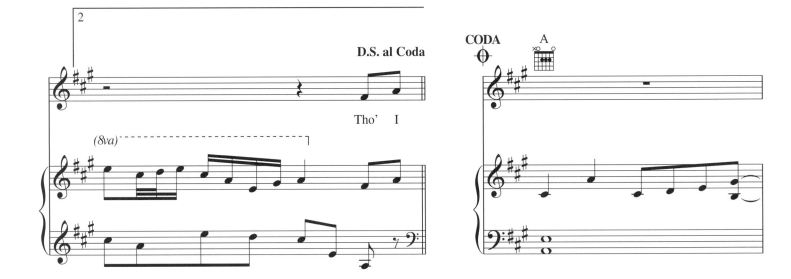

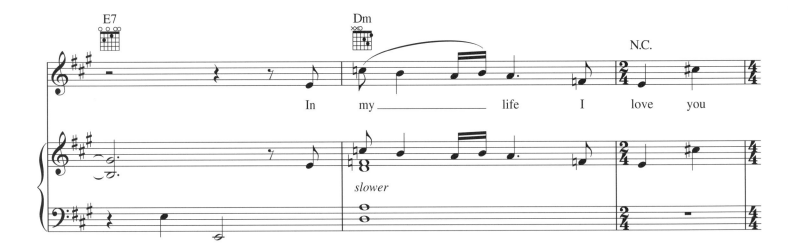

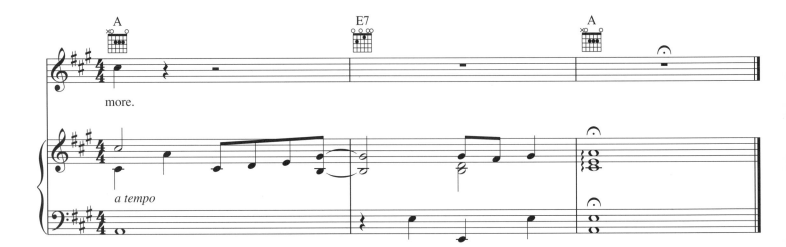

IT'S ONLY LOVE

Words and Music by JOHN LENNON
and PAUL McCARTNEY

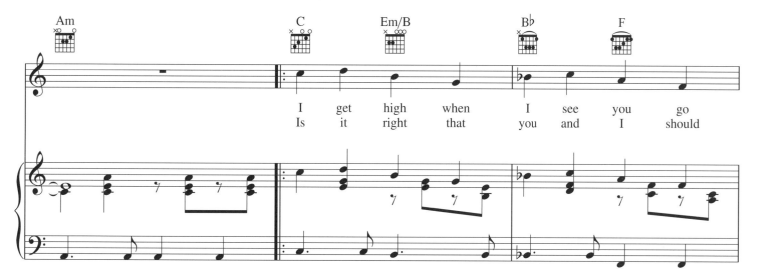

Copyright © 1965 Sony/ATV Music Publishing LLC
Copyright Renewed
All Rights Administered by Sony/ATV Music Publishing LLC, 8 Music Square West, Nashville, TN 37203
International Copyright Secured   All Rights Reserved

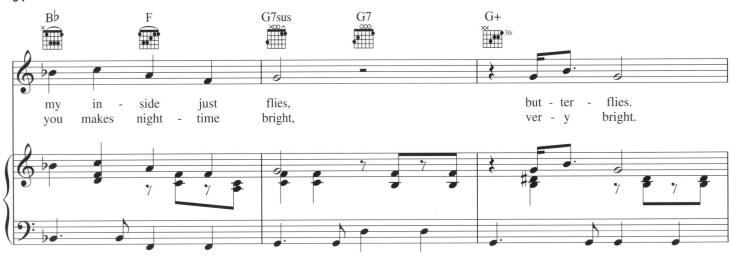

my in - side just flies, but - ter - flies.
you makes night - time bright, ver - y bright.

Why am I so shy when I'm be - side _____ you?
Have - n't I the right to make it up, _____ girl?

It's on - ly love and that is all. ____ Why should I feel ____

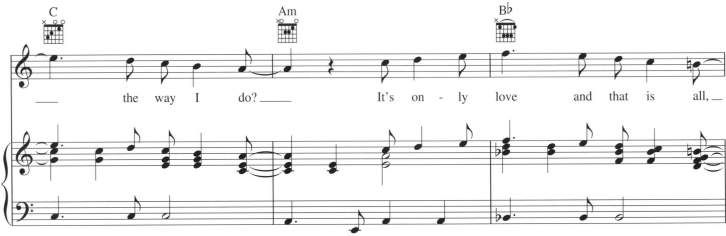

____ the way I do? ____ It's on - ly love and that is all, ____

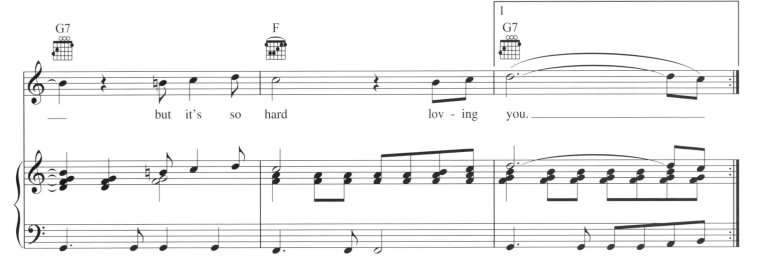

but it's so hard loving you.

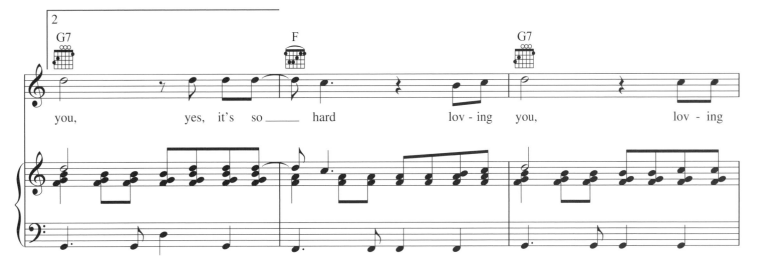

you, yes, it's so ___ hard lov - ing you, lov - ing

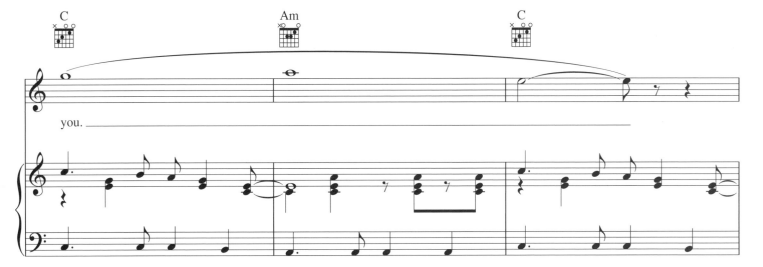

you. ___

JULIA

Words and Music by JOHN LENNON
and PAUL McCARTNEY

Copyright © 1968 Sony/ATV Music Publishing LLC
Copyright Renewed
All Rights Administered by Sony/ATV Music Publishing LLC, 8 Music Square West, Nashville, TN 37203
International Copyright Secured   All Rights Reserved

Her hair of float - ing sky is

shim - mer - ing, glim - mer - ing,

in the sun.

Ju - li - a,

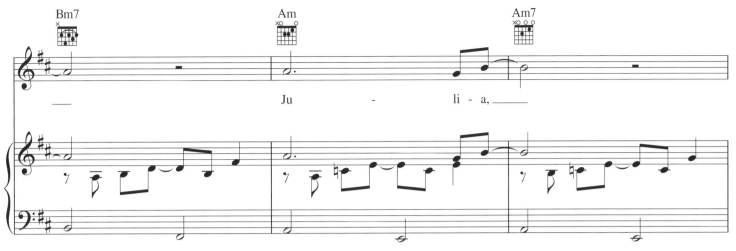

Ju - li - a, ____

morn - ing moon, touch

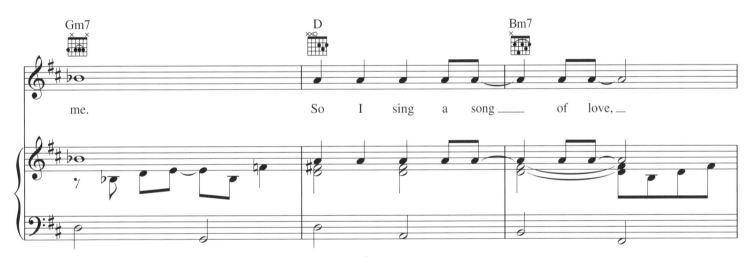

me. So I sing a song ____ of love, ____

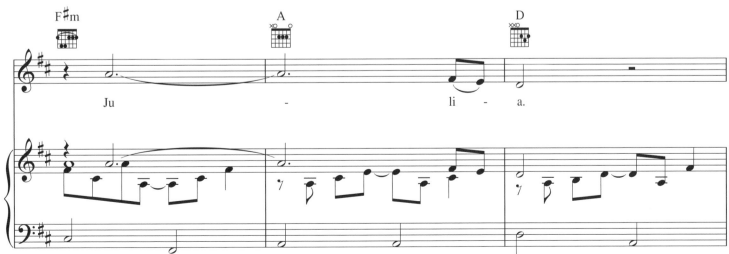

Ju - li - a.

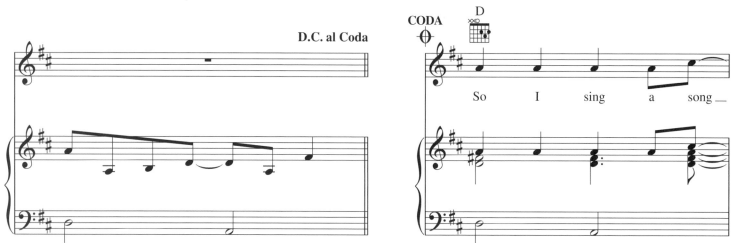

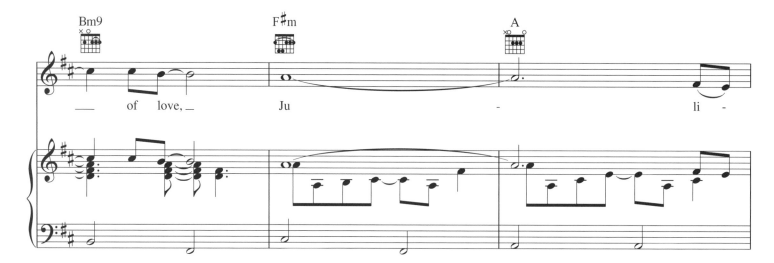

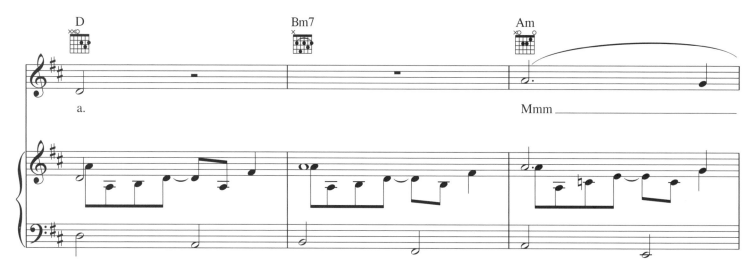

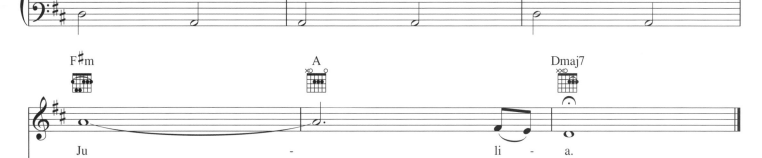

THE LONG AND WINDING ROAD

Words and Music by JOHN LENNON
and PAUL McCARTNEY

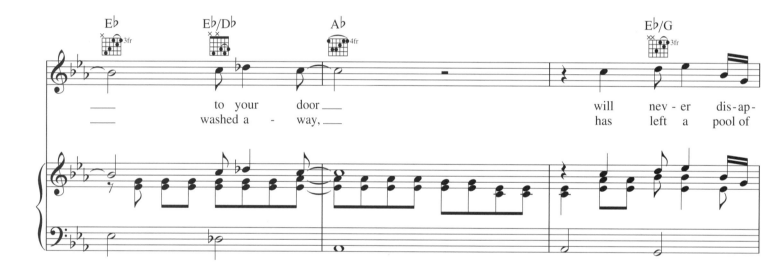

Copyright © 1970 Sony/ATV Music Publishing LLC
Copyright Renewed
All Rights Administered by Sony/ATV Music Publishing LLC, 8 Music Square West, Nashville, TN 37203
International Copyright Secured   All Rights Reserved

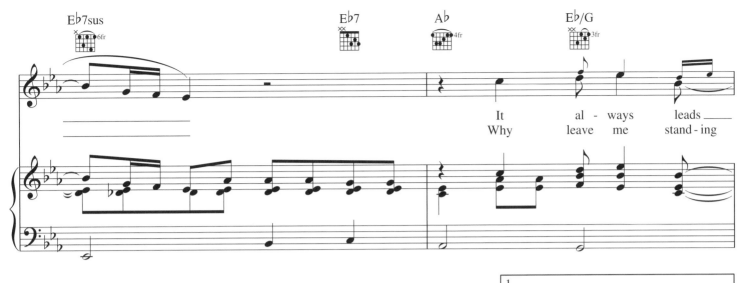

man - y ways __ I've tried. __ And still they lead me back __

__ to the long, __ wind - ing road. __

__ You left me stand - ing here

a long, long time a - go. __

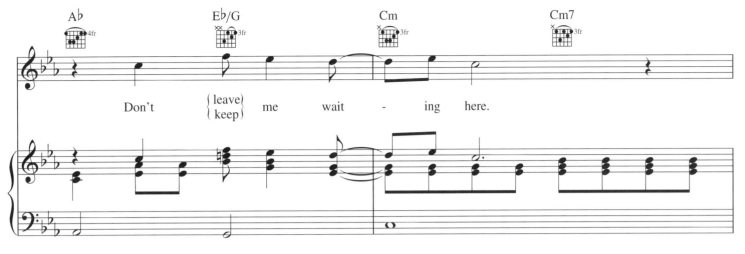

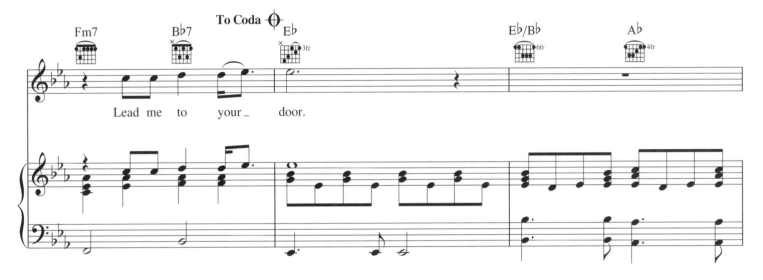

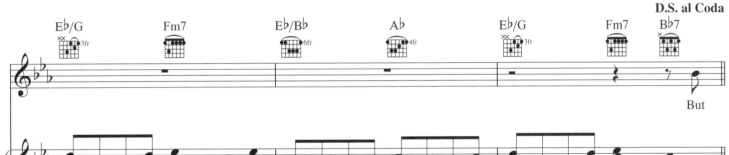

LOVE ME DO

Words and Music by JOHN LENNON
and PAUL McCARTNEY

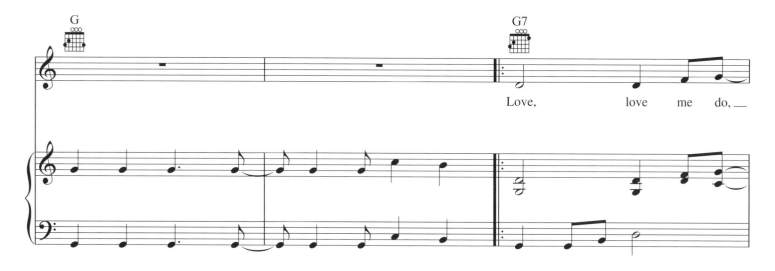

Love, love me do, ___

___ you know I love you. ___ I'll

© 1962, 1963 MPL COMMUNICATIONS LTD.
© Renewed 1990, 1991 MPL COMMUNICATIONS LTD. and LENONO.MUSIC
All Rights for MPL COMMUNICATIONS LTD. in the U.S. and Canada Controlled and Administered by BEECHWOOD MUSIC CORP.
All Renewal Rights for LENONO.MUSIC in the U.S. Controlled and Administered by EMI BLACKWOOD MUSIC INC.
All Rights Reserved   International Copyright Secured   Used by Permission

al - ways be true, _____ so please _____

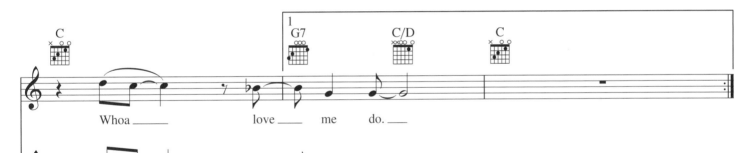

love me do. _____

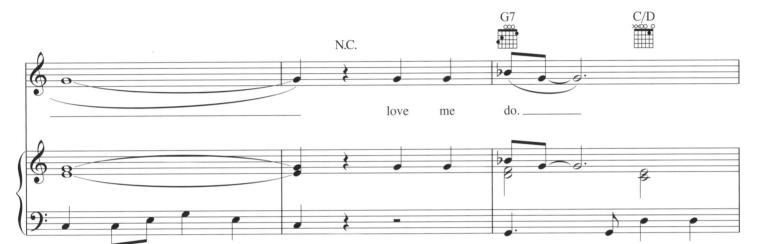

Whoa _____ love _____ me do. _____

_____ me do. _____ Some - one to

Instrumental

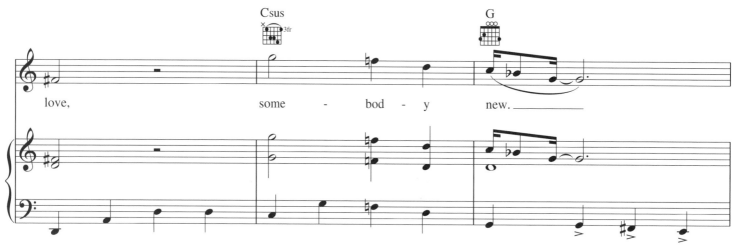

love, some - bod - y new. _____

Some - one to love, some - one like

you. *End instrumental* Love, love me do, _____ you

know I love you. _____ I'll al - ways be true, _

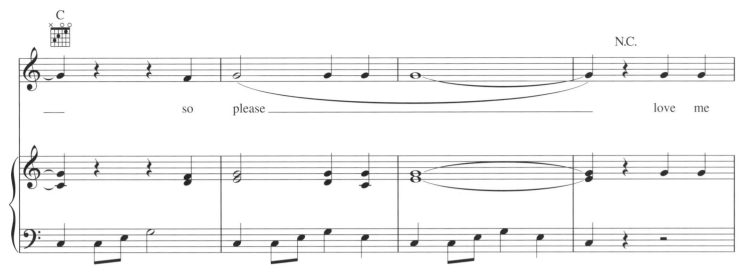

MICHELLE

Words and Music by JOHN LENNON
and PAUL McCARTNEY

Copyright © 1965 Sony/ATV Music Publishing LLC
Copyright Renewed
All Rights Administered by Sony/ATV Music Publishing LLC, 8 Music Square West, Nashville, TN 37203
International Copyright Secured   All Rights Reserved

semble. And I will say the on - ly words ___ I know that

you'll un - der - stand my Mi - chelle.

Repeat and Fade

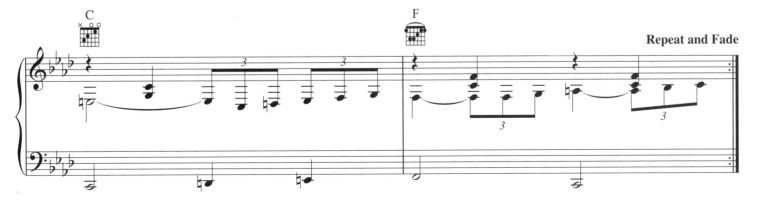

P.S. I LOVE YOU

Words and Music by JOHN LENNON
and PAUL McCARTNEY

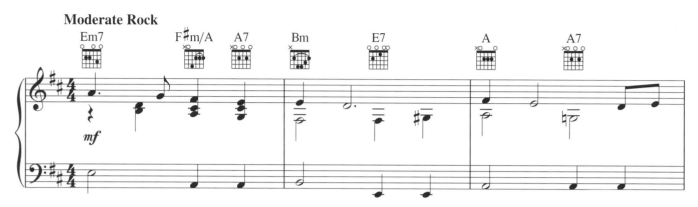

As I write this let - ter,

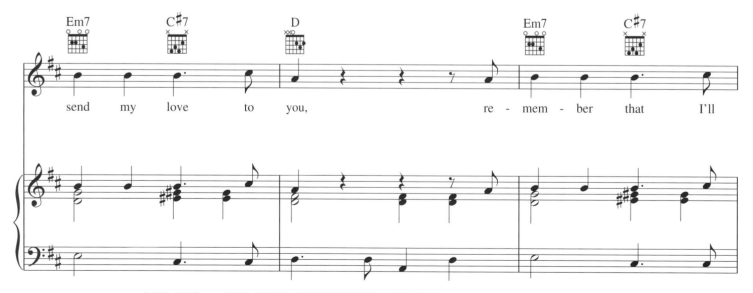

send my love to you, re - mem - ber that I'll

© 1962, 1963 (Renewed 1990, 1991) MPL COMMUNICATIONS LTD., JULIAN LENNON, SEAN ONO LENNON and YOKO ONO LENNON
All Rights for the U.S. Controlled and Administered by BEECHWOOD MUSIC CORP., JULIAN LENNON, SEAN ONO LENNON and YOKO ONO LENNON
All Rights for Canada Controlled and Administered by BEECHWOOD MUSIC CORP.
All Rights Reserved   International Copyright Secured   Used by Permission

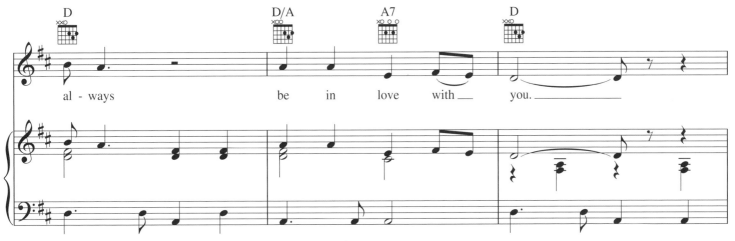

al - ways   be   in love with __ you. ____

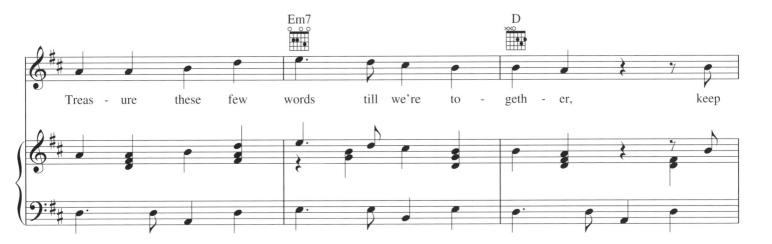

Treas - ure these few words till we're to - geth - er,   keep

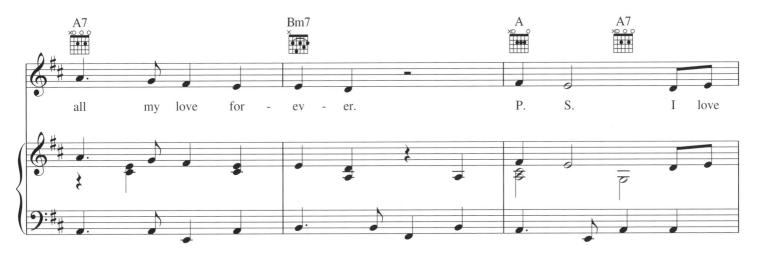

all   my   love for - ev - er.   P.   S.   I   love

you, _____   you, __ you, __ you. ____

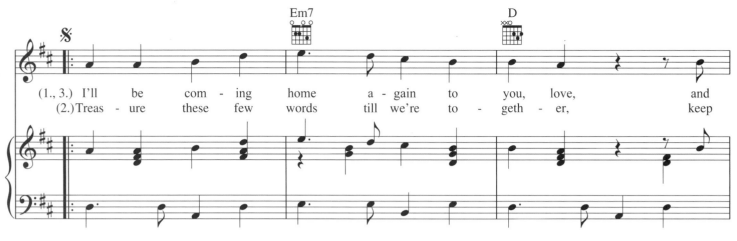

(1., 3.) I'll be com - ing home a - gain to you, love, and
(2.) Treas - ure these few words till we're to - geth - er, keep

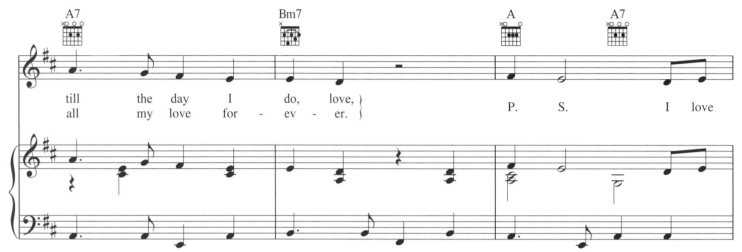

till the day I do, love,
all my love for - ev - er.
P. S. I love

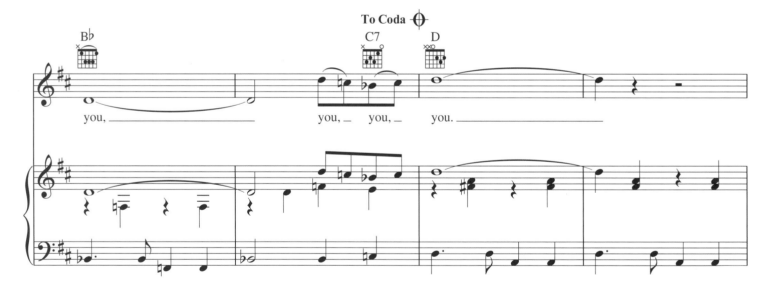

To Coda

you, you, you, you.

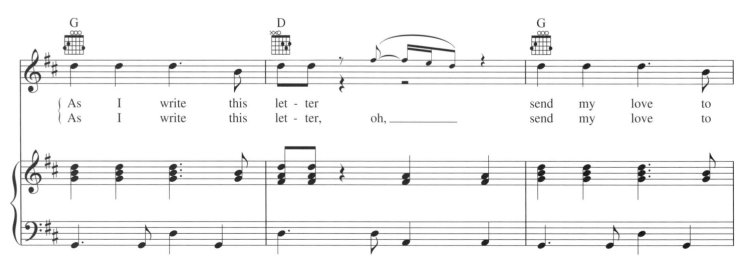

As I write this let - ter send my love to
As I write this let - ter, oh, send my love to

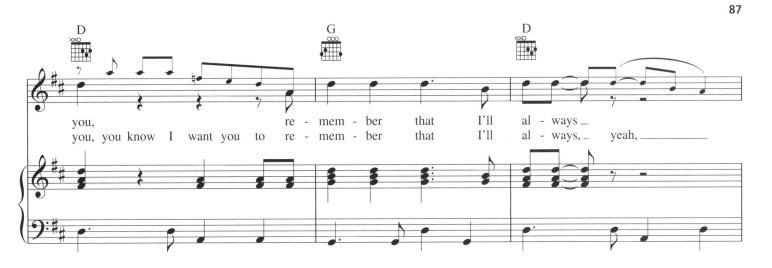

you,   re - mem - ber that I'll al - ways__
you, you know I want you to re - mem - ber that I'll al - ways,__ yeah,_____

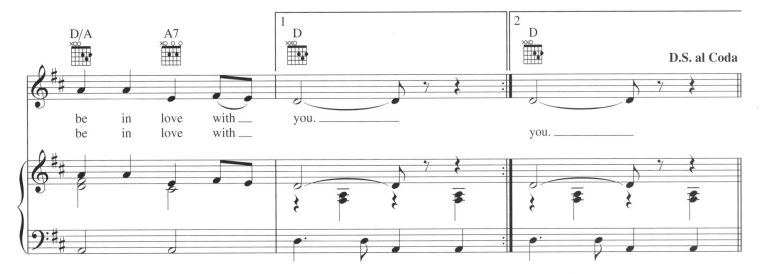

be in love with __ you._____
be in love with __   you._____

you,_____   you, __ you, __ you,_____

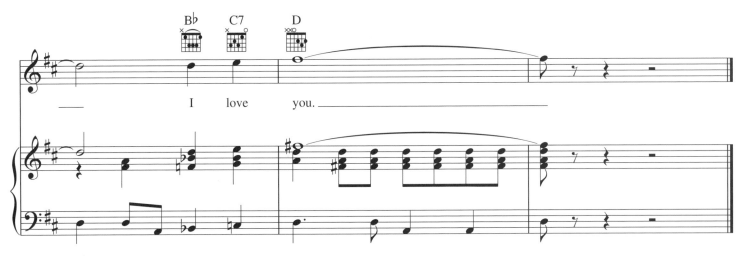

__ I love you._____

SOMETHING

Words and Music by
GEORGE HARRISON

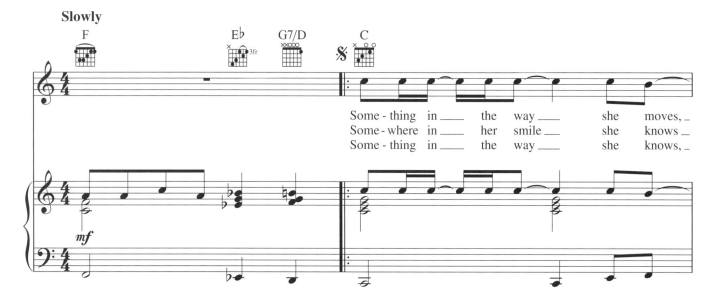

Something in ___ the way ___ she moves, ___
Some-where in ___ her smile ___ she knows ___
Some-thing in ___ the way ___ she knows, ___

at - tracts ___ me like ___ no oth-er lov - er.
that I ___ don't need ___ no oth-er lov - er.
and all ___ I have ___ to do is think ___ of her.

Some-thing in ___ the way ___ she woos ___ me. ___
Some-thing in ___ her style ___ that shows ___ me. ___
Some-thing in ___ the things ___ she shows ___ me. ___

I don't want to leave ___ her now, ___ you

Copyright © 1969 HARRISONGS Ltd.
Copyright Renewed 1998
All Rights Reserved

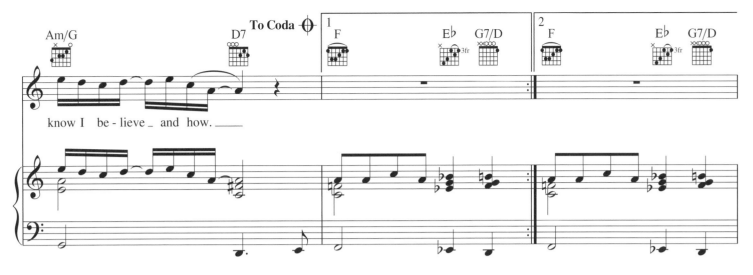

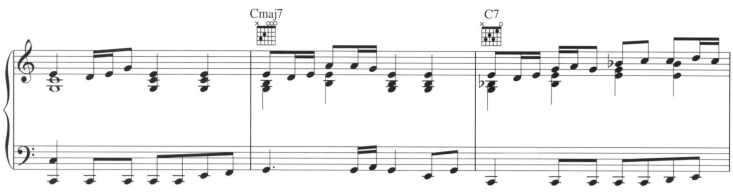

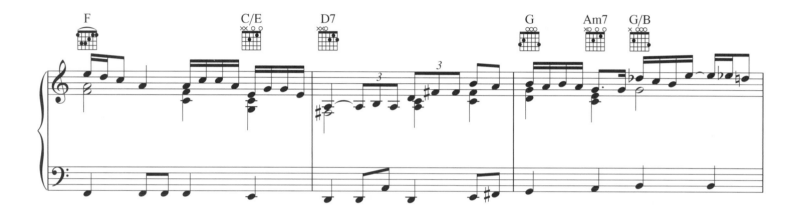

D.S. al Coda

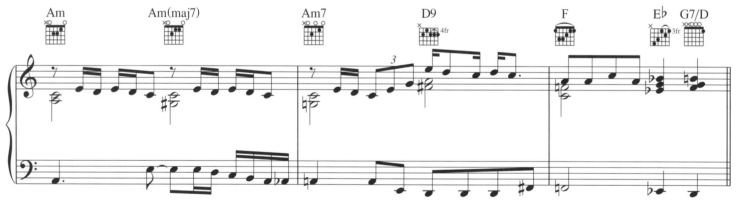

THANK YOU GIRL

Words and Music by JOHN LENNON
and PAUL McCARTNEY

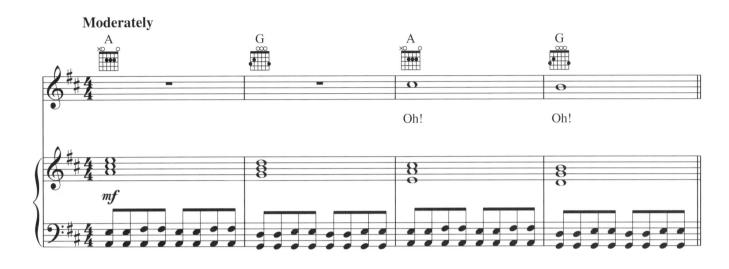

Copyright © 1963 (Renewed) Conrad Music (BMI)
Conrad Music Administered in the United States and Canada by BMG Chrysalis
International Copyright Secured   All Rights Reserved
Used by Permission

be _____ in love with you. _____
fool _____ would doubt our love. _____ And all I got-ta

do _____ is thank you, girl, ___ thank you, girl. ___

Thank you, girl, for lov - in' me the way that you do.

(Way that you do) That's the kind of love that is too good to be true.

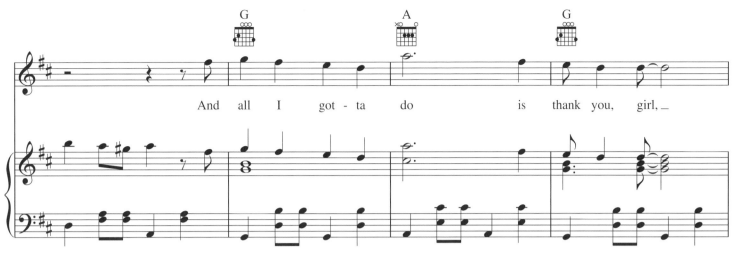

And all I got-ta do is thank you, girl, _

D.C. al Coda (with repeat)

thank you, girl, _

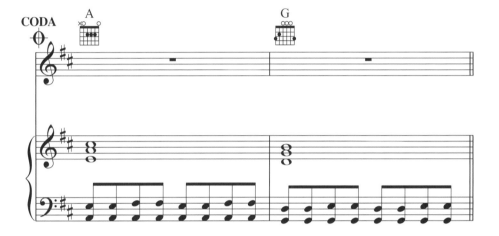

CODA

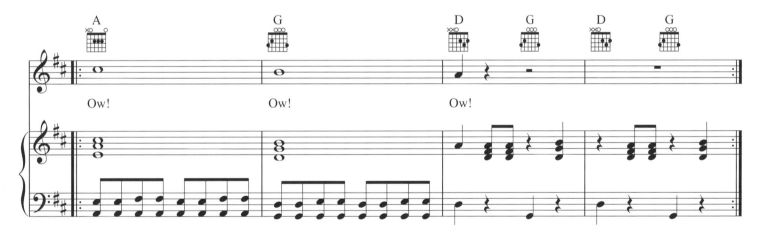

Ow! Ow! Ow!

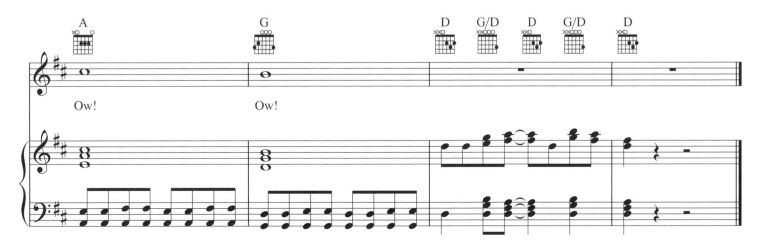

Ow! Ow!

YESTERDAY

Words and Music by JOHN LENNON
and PAUL McCARTNEY

Moderately, with expression

Yes - ter - day, _____ all my trou - bles seemed so
Sud - den - ly, _____ I'm not half the man I

far a - way, _____ now it looks as though _ they're
used to be, _____ there's a shad - ow hang - ing

Copyright © 1965 Sony/ATV Music Publishing LLC
Copyright Renewed
All Rights Administered by Sony/ATV Music Publishing LLC, 8 Music Square West, Nashville, TN 37203
International Copyright Secured   All Rights Reserved

here to stay, ___ oh I be-lieve ___ in yes-ter-day. ___
o-ver me, ___ oh yes-ter-day ___ came sud-den-ly. ___

Why she had to go I don't know, she would-n't say. ___

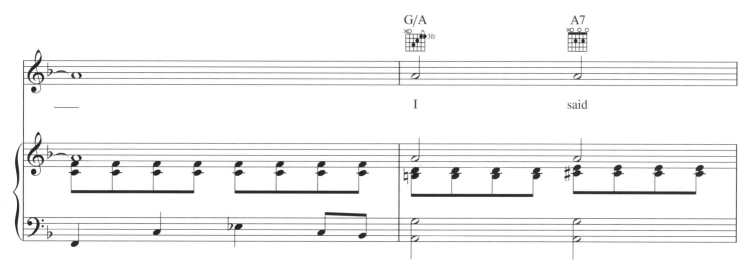

I said

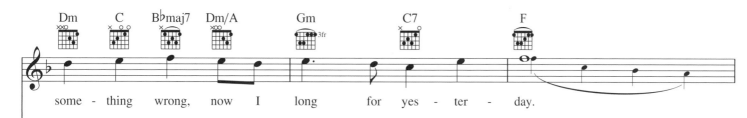

some-thing wrong, now I long for yes-ter-day.

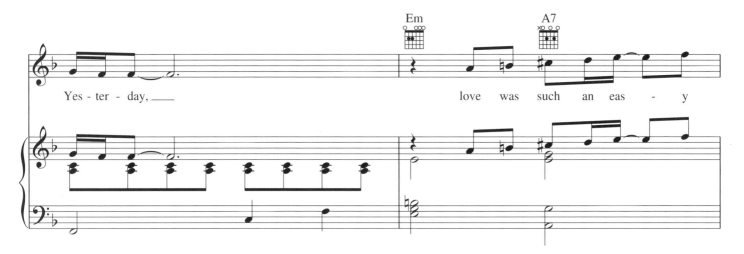

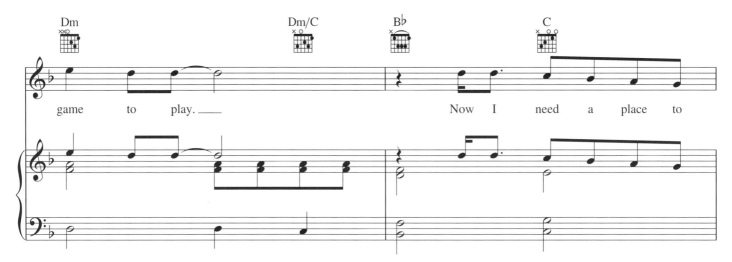

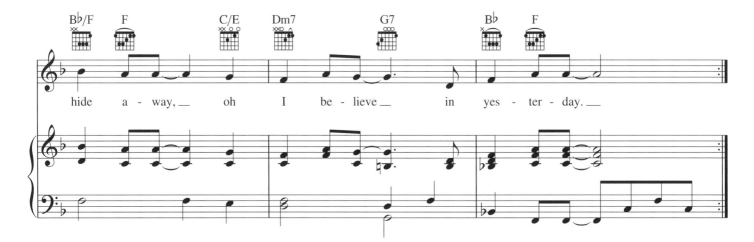

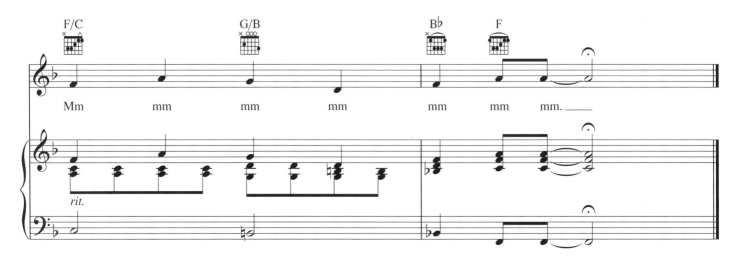